DENNIS KELLY
PLAYS ONE

Dennis Kelly

PLAYS ONE

DEBRIS
OSAMA THE HERO
AFTER THE END
LOVE AND MONEY

OBERON BOOKS
LONDON

First published in this collection in 2008 by Oberon Books Ltd
521 Caledonian Road, London N7 9RH
Tel: 020 7607 3637 / Fax: 020 7607 3629
e-mail: info@oberonbooks.com
www.oberonbooks.com

Reprinted 2009, 2010, 2011

Debris first published 2004, *Osama the Hero* and *After the End* first
published 2005, *Love and Money* first published 2006 by Oberon
Books Ltd.

A catalogue record for this book is available from the British
Library.

Cover photograph from Stock.XCHNG (www.sxc.hu)

ISBN: 978-1-84002-803-4

Printed in Great Britain by CPI Antony Rowe, Chippenham

Contents

DEBRIS

Characters

MICHAEL

MICHELLE

Debris was first performed at Theatre503 (as the Latchmere Theatre) in April 2003, with the following cast:

MICHAEL, Daniel Harcourt
MICHELLE, Carolyn Tomkinson

Director Tessa Walker
Designer Sophie Charalambous
Lighting Phil Hewit

CRUXICIDE

MICHAEL: On my sixteenth birthday my father erected a
   fourteen-foot crucifix in our living room, despite the fact
   that the living room is only eight foot tall. He considers
   smashing a hole through, but – realising that this would
   take away from the dramatic effect – decides that the
   entire ceiling has to go, and so sets to work with a Kango
   hammer on a cleverly constructed trolley, chunks of
   ceiling, dust and carpet from the upstairs flat falling about
   his shoulders like rain and dandruff. He attaches foot-long
   bars horizontally to the back of the cross, which are then
   bolted into the wall, giving the effect of the structure being
   freestanding. It's an impressive sight, which is perhaps
   only slightly marred by the badly framed reproductions of
   spitfires and puppies behind him, and the shockingly dirty
   wallpaper of the flat above.

   The foot-ledge is six foot in the air, and my dad – fond
   of his bacon and eggs – is a fat bastard. Yet somehow he
   makes it. Once up there he is faced with the problem
   of staying on, the foot-ledge being small and at a forty-
   five degree angle, but Daddy, practical as ever, has
   thought ahead and at torso level two leather straps await.
   He buckles himself in, naked, and he pulls on a plastic
   tag – like the American police use – and his left arm is
   secured to the beam. Then… Then he pulls on a lever,
   and the scaffold, the cleverest part of all this, slowly wheels
   into position. He slips his right hand through a tag on that
   side of the beam and somehow manages to give it a pull,
   though obviously it is not as secure as the other one.

   The scaffold. This construction, this ballet of cleverly put
   together levers, pulleys, ropes and sellotape slowly moves
   forward on tracks, the way having been painstakingly
   cleared of rubble and splintered furniture beforehand.
   Once in place it stops, quivering slightly, but ready for
   action. Four wooden tags stick out at the height of my
   father's mouth painted blue, red, yellow and green (I later

found that the paint was harmless if ingested – a touching gesture). These tags have been made from ice-lolly sticks, and if you look on the bottom you can still read the jokes. I didn't though.

It's time. My dad, firmly secured to his masterpiece, cranes his neck and grabs the blue tag with his teeth. Perhaps this was the moment of doubt, perhaps this was the moment of fear, but he jerked that tag back anyway. Levers clicked, ropes tightened, balls rolled, a frog leapt into a bucket and the trigger of the nail gun poised over the palm of his left hand was pulled, slamming a six inch nail through his flesh and into the beam of the cross.

He screams.

Fuck! That hurt, that really hurt! Imagine the shock on my daddy's face as a fix of pain slams into his brain. Flesh rips, the delicate bones of the palm are pushed aside and splintered as a blasphemous intrusion of steel screams through his hand. Imagine him panting, gasping, muttering to himself, sobbing. Imagine him pulling the red tag – you can't? Well he does, he does and his right hand is nailed to the beam.

He screams.

Surely this is enough. Don't you think that this is enough? No Daddy, please, no more, not the yellow tag Pop, please Daddy, you're scaring me – Daddy no! But yes! He pulls it and an extra large nail smashes through the bones of both feet, impaling them to that forty-five degree foot-ledge and making the crucifixion complete. There is silence now apart from the irregular breathing of my dad and the drip of his blood onto the floor.

After what seems like an age my father pulls himself together and goes for that green tag. He slowly reaches out, grabs it with his teeth, and with what's left of his strength he pulls it back. A pin is loosened, the scaffold wobbles for a second, then falls back with a crump and a dramatic billow of dust.

Pause.

Four hours later the living room door is pushed open and I walk in. No presents, no ice cream, no jelly, no vodka, no spotty teens being misunderstood, no screaming children singing happy birthday, just a pile of rubble, scaffold, and my dad dying on the cross. My sixteenth birthday. My coming of age. I hesitantly pick my way through the disaster area, as my father, slowly surfacing from the agony that has become his world, looks down on me. He is very pale. Almost blue. His glistening white body looks like it is made of dough. At some point the contents of his bowels had sprayed themselves across the back of his legs and the upright of the crucifix. He wheezes and gurgles, his lungs filled with fluid, and snot, sweat and spittle dribble down his fat chops. His penis has been made tiny by adrenaline and pain, and the weight of him seems to have stretched the holes in his feet.

Now my old man is not stupid. Think of what he's constructed, think of what he's achieved, think of his eye for detail – think of the paint. He knows exactly how long it takes to die on the cross. He knows exactly what time I will open the door. I'm not saying it's a cry for help, I'm not saying it's a prank that went wrong, I'm not saying that it was an accusatory gesture, but what I am saying is that when I looked into his eyes they were not the eyes of a suicide.

Looking at me now he musters the last remnants of his strength. This is it, this is the moment, the crowning glory of his achievement: he must find it within himself, he must, he must. His head lifts millimetre by millimetre, his mouth opens, dribble and bile spattering to the ground, and from somewhere within that body comes a voice, a sound, a sentence:

'My son, my son, why have you forsaken me?'

And as these words leave the air his head rolls onto his chest. There. He's done it. It's over. Now he can rest. It's over.

So he thinks. I look at him. Surely this wasn't how Jesus looked? Surely Our Lord had a bit more style, a bit more élan, a bit more pizzazz. He looks utterly disgusting up there on his fourteen-foot crucifix, his head in the home of another flat, his feet in ours. He thinks it's over. But it's not.

'Forgive me father, for I know not what I do.'

And with that I carefully back away. I'm almost at the door before the meaning of this has got through his pain. I watch it trickle through his brain, and suddenly he looks at me in absolute terror.

Slowly, I leave, closing the door behind me.

THE LAST CHICKEN ON EARTH

MICHELLE: My mother died of Joy. On the day that I was born, while I sat there hanging in my mother's fluid, suspended in aspic, my thumb in my mouth, my mother and father experienced a wave of joy so profound that as it washed over them and frothed on their skins they instinctively knew that not to find expression for this heat would mean the end of all three of us, the fabric of our bodies collapsing on a molecular level in the face of such extremes of energy and so my dad cooked a chicken. He had seen this on TV. A man cooking a chicken. He had to do this because of the bundle of life wrapped up in my mother's belly – me, yes me – a mess of skin, flesh, bone, placenta and God's holy bounty about to become detached and walk amongst them bringing happiness and purpose to their lives. That was how they felt. It was. You can imagine their irritating smiles as they sat in expectant silence, this ever expanding growth of chromosomes rendering words useless, occasionally catching each other's eye and laughing like streams, my dad capering now into the kitchen, if a sixteen-stone man who in all probability was pissed can be said to caper.

Chicken was definitely the answer. When this man on the telly cooked chicken you could tell that he understood joy, you could tell that that man there was life, that man there with the chicken, that man that understood joy, that man there on the telly cooking that chicken who understood joy, that man there, that there, that there was life and my dad knew that, which is why he cooked a chicken for my mum, just like that man there on the telly because of joy, and the joy was me, I was the joy, you see, I was the joy. Me. I was their joy.

My dad brings in the chicken in triumph, held high above his head like a cooked chicken held high above his head and deep down on my mother's liver I experience the thrill of expectation that races through her bloodstream, hear the gentle flutter of butterflies' wings near my ear, and can't help but feel caught up in this general feeling that things are going to be good, that fortune is smiling, that God is handing out lollies and I grin to myself around my now fully-formed thumb and kick playfully at my mother's spleen. They begin to eat the chicken, which is, to be honest, a little dry and overcooked, but they begin to eat the chicken as if it were the last chicken on earth, grinning at each other through the grease on their chins and occasionally tossing a half-eaten wing to my brother who lies in the corner paddling around in his own excrement, though in all fairness he was, unlike me, a mistake and not wanted and it all sort of went horribly wrong with him so you can hardly blame them for wanting to start again, so maybe you shouldn't think about him, so forget what I said about him, okay, he's not there.

And then a bone gets caught in my mother's throat and she begins to die. A little cough and they giggle at this teasing burp, shovelling more chicken down their gullets, my father swallowing, my mother dying. A halting wheeze and again they giggle though my mother betrays an ounce of uncertainty as she winkles flesh from a tiny rib with her left incisor. And then she's waving, choking, pointing at her back and clutching her throat, still clinging to her chicken but unable to breath. My dad, still consumed with joy, gambols around behind her and gives her a playful tap on the neck, but seeing her lips turn blue begins to panic, to roar, to scream, punches her in the back of the head, desperate to dislodge the obstruction, while I, caught up in the panic, push my groping arm pointlessly upwards, Dad smacking her in the back of the head with his shovel, bellowing at God, my child, my child, my wife and my child.

My mother now staggers around the room like a dying dinosaur about to fall on a car and suddenly in a flash of inspiration my dad remembers the Heimlich manoeuvre and grabs my mother around the waist, his fists clamping around my neck like a meat scarf, tensing, ready, flexing, about to…

'NO!'

Coughs my mother with the last wisps of her breath and wrenches herself from his grasp spinning around to face him, her hands wrapped protectively on what she thought was my head but was in fact her pancreas. They stare at each other, knowing. Realising. My father almost blind with panic, my mother calming him with her gaze as her life bleeds away, somehow making him understand that they had to choose, me or her, and they chose me, you see, they chose me, through the pain and the anguish and the tears and despair they chose me, and my mother died there in my father's arms as his soul exploded and the TV found itself crashing through the window and smashing into the concrete four floors below.

And they chose me.

It was very touching.

It was.

Very.

Very touching.

It was.

DIVORCE

MICHAEL: This boy…this boy in this pizza place I was looking
at through this window, I was looking at this boy through
this window, staring at this boy who sat opposite this
man in a suit, the only communication the boy flicking
his olives onto the man's pizza, the man eating them, the
man spitting the stones into the palm of his hand, the
hand placing them in the metal ashtray with a soft click
where they sat like wide-eyed children watching this silent
production line, waiting for their parents to speak, I had
seen…this before. Where? Where had I seen this before?
I stayed and watched. I followed, I followed them, when
they left I followed them but at a discreet distance through
many twisting streets, past shops and then hedges, trees,
low walls and doors that were all different from each
other. They went into the house, up to, they went up to the
house, up to the, the man pushed the buzzer, the boy got
out a key, and the door opened before the key was…before
he could…with the key, he… It was a woman, of course,
she hugged the boy who went inside and they talked, the
man and woman, irritated, I think she was a little irritated
but they kissed goodbye like aunts and the man went
away, where had I seen this before? I stayed. I watched.
I looked in through the windows. I saw the boy watching
TV. I saw the mother talking, talking on the phone. I saw a
glass of wine. I saw cooked vegetables. I saw her hair. I saw
homework. I saw pyjamas. I saw him talking, talking on
the phone. I saw him talking to her. I saw. I saw. And

I

Saw

Him

Lying

In her

Lap.

I had seen this before. Through windows of TV shops I had seen this on TVs through the windows of TV shops before, I had seen this before, this was how people, perhaps this was how people lived.

Pause.

I broke in through a very small toilet window, quite high up, but not so high that I couldn't reach, the atmosphere immediately different, the smell of other people, the sound of the TV, the warmth of the air all crowding around and brushing my skin like her hair. I crept gently and quietly forward into the living room and crouched between the door and the couch, her and her boy sitting there, his head in her lap, her hands stroking his head and them watching TV. I listened to their talk. I smelled her shampoos and soaps. I watched telly inches away from them, sitting there crouched at the end of their sofa, listening to their talk and purrs and all three of us were happy, oh yes, we were, we were all three happy.

Pause.

The scream ripped through my flesh like a nail fired from a gun, imbedding itself in the delicate bones of my inner ear so that if I concentrate I can still hear it there now. For one tiny endless eggshell second we all three hovered there facing each other, not wanting to move in case the moment shattered like glass. Then she hurled her son, the boy, through the door, the kitchen, the kitchen door which leads to the kitchen, where there was a phone, in the kitchen there was a phone and she pushed her son through that door, following herself, while I ran for the other one, the one at the front of the house the front door. I belted away into the night, the scream hurting, water blinding, snot choking, ran, I ran, I ran fast and hard away and there was a siren, behind me, a siren was behind me, fast, I ran fast, the scream there in my ear in in my heart, I ran and looked left, right, somewhere to hide from the scream behind me, so I turned into flats, an estate, though the car was still behind, in the estate, I was running on an estate – or in an estate – running, turning, the siren/scream with me everywhere, one turn a door open I jumped in, into smell, just bad smell a where people throw their, down a chute into a where people chuck their thrown away into a pile rubbish, a pile of rubbish, in the in the in the in the in the, a pile of rubbish, in the in the in the in the in the, a pile of rubbish, in the.

Pause.

About half an hour later I heard a rustle beside me.

UNCLEARRY

MICHAEL is strangling MICHELLE, who is kneeling on the floor, her face turning red, then purple, then blue. It is taking a huge amount of effort and goes on for some time. Slowly he looks up and still trying with all his might to crush his sister's neck, he speaks through clenched teeth.

MICHAEL: Killing my sister was proving almost impossible, due to the tenacity with which she clung to her life.

Suddenly he lets go of her, exhausted. She collapses on the floor, gasping, coughing and rubbing her neck. He puts his hands into his armpits as if they were burnt. There is a long silence. MICHAEL shakes his hands and blows on them, and then puts them under his arms again.

Fuck!

MICHELLE: (*Her voice a croak.*) You swore.

MICHAEL: What?

MICHELLE: You shouldn't swear.

MICHAEL: Sorry.

Long pause.

My hands hurt.

MICHELLE slowly climbs to her feet, unsteady and coughing. She crosses over to her brother, takes his hands in hers and begins to rub them. He winces.

MICHELLE: Don't be such a baby.

Shamed, he allows her to rub the life back into his hands. He feels better.

It's your own fault.

MICHAEL: I have to kill you.

MICHELLE: No you don't.

MICHAEL: I do!

MICHELLE: Who said?

MICHAEL: He won't take both of us.

MICHELLE: (*To the audience.*) That's not true.

(*To MICHAEL.*) That's not true.

MICHAEL: (*To MICHELLE.*) It is!

(*To the audience.*) It is!

MICHELLE: You see the problem was that I'd got a little upset when UncleArry –

MICHAEL: Who isn't really our uncle.

MICHELLE: Better than an uncle.

MICHAEL: Much better.

MICHELLE: – had stolen us.

MICHAEL: Rescued us.

MICHELLE: Alright, rescued us. But that's only natural.

MICHAEL: You wanna go back?

MICHELLE: Fuck off!

They are both shocked. Pause.

MICHAEL: You blubbed like a baby.

MICHELLE: I was cold. I was scared. We'd been sitting outside the Crown and Goose for fourteen hours with no more to sustain us than a lemonade each and a pack of Monster Munch.

MICHAEL: At last Dad came out.

MICHELLE: His arm 'round UncleArry.

MICHAEL: Vomit down his shirt making him look like he'd had his throat cut.

MICHELLE: Dad's conversion to Catholicism had been hotly followed by the customary Jesus fixation, and now he drank nothing but water and wine.

MICHAEL: Though mostly wine.

MICHELLE: They both looked at us and UncleArry says:

MICHAEL: Those yours?

MICHELLE: In reply, Daddy, never a man of many words, farted loudly and fell flat on his face.

MICHAEL: You're a lucky man, my friend.

MICHELLE: Said UncleArry, but by this time Daddy was already in the land of nod.

'Ow old are ya?

MICHAEL: Twelve, I said.

MICHELLE: Nine and three quarters.

MICHAEL: Said my sister, squeezing out every month she could get. He looked at us long and hard.

MICHELLE: What lovely ages you 'ave.

MICHAEL: And suddenly, UncleArry –

MICHELLE: Not before taking Dad's wallet.

MICHAEL: For petrol he said.

MICHELLE: – grabbed us both, stuck us in his car, and sped off into the cold December night.

MICHAEL: And that's when you started blubbing.

MICHELLE: Which prompted UncleArry to nudge him in the ribs and through a cloud of Johnnywalkerfaggarlicgas utter:

MICHAEL: Girls, eh? What can we do with 'em?

MICHELLE: But that don't mean you should kill me!

MICHAEL: What else can I do? You wanna go back to the Crown and Goose?

MICHELLE: But what about Mister Bought and Smite?

MICHAEL: He won't take you.

MICHELLE: That's not fair!

MICHAEL: I'm sorry.

MICHELLE: I want to live with Mister Bought and Smite as well! I want to live in a big house with ice cream and servants and champagne.

MICHAEL: You don't even know what champagne is.

She sits down to sulk. During this speech MICHAEL crosses to get a cup and then brings it back to his sister.

And so she went on. But what she couldn't see was the look that UncleArry had given me when we was in the car, when he had said that about girls. Though hideously ugly in his stained tweed jacket and diamond cut jumper, though drooling and smelling of piss, I could tell he was a kind man – he had to be, otherwise why rescue us from our lives? That look on a more lowly human being might have been mistaken for greed, for avarice, for lascivious hunger, for vulturious lust, but on that kind and saintly man I knew he was worried that his good deed would come a cropper because she was a Girl.

He hands the cup to MICHELLE who is rubbing her throat.

MICHELLE: Ta.

She takes a gulp and immediately spits it out. She starts coughing and gasping.

MICHAEL: Drink it: it's good for you.

MICHELLE: What is it?

MICHAEL: Bleach.

MICHELLE: Bleach?

MICHAEL: Yeah. It'll kill ya.

MICHELLE: (*Throwing the cup down.*) I don't wanna be killed!

Long pause.

And so we waited. I was sure he was wrong, otherwise why would UncleArry take me as well? Why not leave me there with my Daddy, waiting for the sun to rise over the Crown and Goose like a hangover? Mister Bought and Smite would want a boy and a girl, the poor lonely man.

MICHAEL: I don't wanna go back.

MICHELLE: Me neither.

MICHAEL: This is a dream come true. Like getting something you actually want for Christmas.

MICHELLE: I used to dream of being abducted by aliens.

MICHAEL: Of contracting a rare and highly contagious disease.

MICHELLE: Of being adopted.

MICHAEL: Or of being taken into care.

Pause.

Anyone arks ya…

MICHELLE: Says UncleArry.

MICHAEL: An' I'm your UncleArry.

MICHELLE: Which is stupid coz that's who he was.

MICHAEL: And do as I fucking well tell ya!

MICHELLE: UncleArry's tone had changed as he got out of the car and headed towards a derelict slum.

MICHAEL: Must be the pressure. Poor man.

MICHELLE: And then he locked us in a room.

MICHAEL: I gots calls to make.

MICHELLE: And with that he was off. And so we waited.

Pause. They wait.

UncleArry bursts in, breathless and excited and smelling like a drunken cabbage, his lips curl back and expose his rotten teeth and at first we flinch but then it slowly dawns on us. He's smiling.

MICHAEL: Good news, good and beautiful news! He's here. The man we've been waiting for, Mr fucking wonderful himself! Now I want you to be good little angels and smile as pretty as you can – cause if you don't…!

(*He smiles again.*) Remember the big house. Remember the ice cream. Remember the servants and champagne. But most of all remember the back of my fucking hand! And if you start blubbing…

(*As himself.*) I knew I should've killed her.

…there'll be hell to pay. Now kiddies, think of nice things and put your hands together for the marvellous, for the fabulous, for the sophisticated, for the stinking fucking rich…

MICHELLE /MICHAEL: (*Together, in wonder as he enters.*) Mister Bought and Smite!

DEBRIS

MICHAEL: I used to believe that babies were found under gooseberry bushes. I had heard that they were delivered by storks, dropped gently down chimneys to land in little white bundles of fluff. I even once believed that we were brought into this world by the miracle of conception, gestation and then childbirth, but I now know that not to be the case. Like mushrooms, babies grow in rubbish. They construct themselves from rotting leaves, coke cans, syringes and empty packets of monster munch and wait for their parents to find them. I know this to be the truth. Because I found one.

Beside me this rustling sound, rustling beside me, in the dark, smell, rustling in, I was still sweating, hiding and beside me there was this rustling in, in the dark and I look down in a shaft from the street light, from the crack in the door I had to push open the door to let in a shaft of street light in a crack so I could see, which cut across the rubbish and illuminated a, a hand, a very small hand. A very small hand. A very small baby. It was a very small baby in the rubbish.

I reach down, my hand, reach with my hand and push aside washing powder boxes and ladies' tights and pull out a very small baby, greens clinging to its head, browns covering its hand and I pull out a very small baby and lift it up a very small naked cold baby, a boy a little boy, and I pull out a very small cold naked baby boy, my boy, my boy I pull out my boy.

What happened inside was an organ in my chest dissolved,
was teleported from me, into me, out of me, turned
to snow, into warmth into golden blood which rushed
through my veins and turned my mind into fire, my
body into blazing scream, laugh, I didn't know what was
– instinct kicked in, inside, instinct burned around my
body like adrenaline, like gin, burned around my body
destroying my mind in a second, in a flash, searing the
shadow of it against the inside of my skull and replacing
it with something else, something new, something very
different, a new, a new…

He was very cold. Dying. He was dying. I sat there for an
hour, I was there for an hour sat in other people's rubbish
with a dying baby in my arms rocking back and forth and
I was happy, oh yes, I was happy. I look down, his lips
are like – ebbing, his life is – slugs, his lips like tiny grey
slugs – fading, his lips moving slightly, little circles made
from his hands in the air surrounding us, floating around
us, tiny ice cubes, he was cold so with my shirt, I opened
my shirt because panic was now pushing its way through,
I was beginning to panic because to find and then lose,
so I opened my shirt I hid him close to me, I wrapped
him in me I dragged him into me into my love, rocking,
close to my heart, the circles becoming smaller now as he
became weaker, though warmth began, it was maybe too
late, I could see his slugs lips, in his lips, weakness, hunger
draining his cold, draining into me, his life draining out of
him, his movements going, leaving him and I pulled him
to me and rocked faster because what else could I do?

And somehow

He finds his way to my breast.

*He screams as the baby bites into him. He gasps with pain and
anguish, still holding the child, writhing but not wanting to
disturb it. He begins to get used to it as he looks down at the
baby.*

And he fed at my breast. Not milk but blood. He slowly
drinks what life he can from my tiny nipple, his grey lips
becoming red, his hand waving, and I feel that surge of
feeling burst through my chest again, flooding my body,
my mind. It's love. Isn't it. It's love. I look down at my
boy, my son, my…my…feeding there, my…my…life
pounding back into him, my…my…Rubbish? Garbage?
Debris. Good name. Sounds French. Be able to get him
into posh schools with a name like that. My Debris.
My Debris.

NECROVIVIPARITY

MICHELLE: No…

My mother died of an observation. The observation was
not hers. She rejected death by overdose, by murder, by
gas explosion, by unsuccessful surgery, by diphtheria, by
typhoid, by stabbing and by old age to die of ennui. Whilst
watching a late night arts programme – not her customary
fare – and eating a jar of pickled onions – her customary
fare – she happened to hear one of the panel remark:

'Of course, it's impossible to create anything original these
days.'

She stops mid-chew, another onion halfway to her mouth,
puts her other hand on her balloon of a stomach, and lets
the ramifications sink in. But she's creating something new,
isn't she? Something original in her belly? That moving
kicking wrapped-up ball of six months flesh, surely that's
original? But she knows. It is not so much the certainty of
the remark itself but the nodding way in which the rest of
those intellectuals and artists greet it, as if it was understood
by everyone in the world. Except my mother.

Her face slowly slackens, the jaw loosening, the cheeks
hollowing, the muscles in the eyes becoming soft as kidney.
Her arm drops and the pickled onion falls, bouncing once,

twice, then rolling to the TV as if taking sides, the little round bastard.

She stares.

For a long time.

The picture on the screen fades into a little dot, turns to fuzz, and then the next morning, bursts into life again and still my mother stares. And, as that night the picture fades again into a pickled onion, so my mum, relinquishing her life, fades into a corpse, leaving that poor defenceless child in her belly – namely me – to fend for herself.

After a brief period of mourning my father pushes my mommy off the couch and onto the floor and switches over to the football. And there I gestate, in my mother's rotting corpse, protected by her womb, three months of my development yet to go, though I take four seeing as how I'd have to go through the birth unaided. This was the most difficult period, as well you might imagine, defying the laws of life and death so that I may one day take my unoriginal place in that unoriginal world. The womb holds up well but toward the end begins to give way to the bacteria so that it has to be patched up with other parts of my mother's anatomy, such as the spleen or a handful of liver, not to mention the odd empty crisp packet that my groping hand finds lying on the floor.

On the first of May I burst forth from between my mother's legs to make my pigheaded and painstaking way towards her breast, but find there a source of sustenance only a plant could find a use for. And so I push my mouth onto that mound of stagnant jelly and allow my lips to take root, my tongue to turn tuber, so as to partake of the goodness that is my birthright. Over the coming months I sprout leaves – which of course I have subsequently shed – that cleverly turn towards the sun, the better to aid photosynthesis. And all that time I eye up the TV. Coz I know. Coz I haven't forgotten. Coz I remember.

Poor Mummy. She had forgotten that the little men are not real, that it's just a magic box, that words are no more than an ever increasingly abstract collection if sounds in the air. The reality was in her belly, the reality was growing inside, the reality was me – plant child sucking death through a potato tongue – that was reality.

I throw out tendrils everywhere to gain more life, my father of course – not being the most affectionate of men – brushes them aside, but mostly I push them towards that glowing box in the corner, towards my foe. It is a painstaking process, taking almost a year, but I get there in the end. Little is left of my mother by this stage, just a few dirty bones and some brown sludge, but the pickled onion is doing surprisingly well soaked as it is in its spicy malt vinegar and hidden from my fat dad by the leg of the telly. Now I crawl to that box, my tendrils slowly closing like a fist I am a snake a boa constrictor a hand a fist around an egg squeezing poised to crush… Suddenly there is a movement behind me. It's Daddy. He has noticed what is going on, not-televisual sight at this desperate moment finally penetrating his meat-head.

'NO!'

He screams.

I stop.

I look round at him.

There is only pain in his face.

Infinite loss. A voice barely audible.

'Not the telly!'

Pause. She reconsiders.

Squeeze.

She screams and falls to the floor.

(*Raising her head*.) He gets up. He looks around. He is like a man possessed released of his demons, blinking in the sunlight. He sees our mum. He sees our dead mum.

Something in my father snapped that day.

TELLY

MICHAEL: So in the dark, out of that rubbish tip, smell, I left, went home, made my way home with, went home with Debris, with my boy, with my boy Debris and my new mind, through the streets but I see nothing, around me there was nothing, nothing around me just a burn held close to my chest, melting, this boy melting the rocks inside, a small tiny cold fire held close to my chest, though not so cold now, not so, not so, not so cold now, the lips, full red lips now, and maybe a smile, I'm not sure, maybe a smile, the smile even the hint of which was enough to stand my hair on end with tiny crackles of blue lightning tracing a path up each fibre to flick and disappear with a seismic tingle through my bones, this was my boy, this was my boy, this was my Debris.

At four in the morning I would crawl from my bed and sleepwalk to the cardboard box where I kept him, to be jolted awake by a stab of pure agony receding into pure love. I bounced him on my knee, and when I burped him little red traces of myself would trickle from his mouth onto my shoulder and a tiny cloud that tasted like guinness would drift into my face. And we were happy. Oh yes. We were happy.

My sister. My sister, I let my sister in on, I had to, I had to let my sister in on this secret, because she would've, she definitely would've found out, and I needed, I needed some help, hiding, hiding him from my dad, and she would help, watching, I felt her watching the boy with me and I felt something else, from her, coming from her, emanating, this feeling of, I couldn't quite make it out as she watched us, but she kept watch and I was able, became able, was able to look after the boy while she watched, and planted an idea in my head.

MICHELLE: You gonna grow him up here?

MICHAEL: Yeah.

MICHELLE: Here?

MICHAEL: Yeah.

MICHELLE: Here?

MICHAEL: Yeah.

MICHELLE: You gonna grow him up here?

MICHAEL: Yes.

Pause.

MICHELLE: We ain't got a telly.

MICHAEL: So?

MICHELLE: They need a telly.

MICHAEL: This was true.

They do. They do need a telly. I looked at us. I looked at the world outside. I looked at him. How could he be like them? How could he move through them? My blood wasn't enough. I left him with my sister while I went out looking for a telly.

MISTER BOUGHT AND SMITE

MICHELLE: (*As Mister Bought and Smite.*) Why what a fabulously charming place you have: how novel to allow your brown floral wallpaper to peel from the brickwork, how clever of you to have covered every conceivable surface with dirt. It's simply so earthy, so bohemian, so wanton, so…*pauvre.* Jeremy Boughton-Smythe at your service, or rather you at mine, you must be Arry.

MICHAEL: …

MICHELLE: To have broken this chair to splinters, to have cracked this decaying plaster, to have smashed all the windows, to have infected this carpet with fleas shows a delicate eye for detail that one cannot help but admire. I'm convinced we shall be firm friends. Is this faecal matter human or animal?

MICHAEL: …

MICHELLE: Ignore me! Forgive my craven display of shallility. When gazing upon the Mona Lisa one does not enquire where Da Vinci brought his paint. You are a rare genius, Arry. I shall compose a poem in your honour at once.

MICHAEL: …

MICHELLE: And this is Guy…

MICHAEL walks forward as Guy.

My gorilla.

(*As herself.*) And the room shrank to the size of a matchbox as the biggest man in the world walked through that door.

MICHAEL: Our mouths dropped.

MICHELLE: Yes I know, he is a trifle crude but you must admit, terribly effective. And he plays the harpsichord like an angel. Now, Arry…

MICHAEL: Sir.

MICHELLE: I believe you have something for me. Or rather some things.

MICHAEL: And UncleArry pushed us toward Mister Bought and Smite.

MICHELLE: Never had we seen anything like it.

MICHAEL: Mister Bought and Smite so clean and crisp that it was painful to look at him.

MICHELLE: And the biggest cruellest man in the world at his shoulder, with eyes that showed he had no thoughts in his tiny brain that were not directed towards his nose, which he was now industriously picking.

(*As Mister Bought and Smite.*) Ah children, children…

MICHAEL: Said Mister Bought and Smite.

MICHELLE: What delightful specimens you are.

MICHAEL: And he pulled out two lollies.

MICHELLE: One for you, my precious young Ganymede…

MICHAEL: Which greedily I took.

MICHELLE: And one for you my delicious little nymphet.

(*As herself.*) Teacher said I shouldn't take sweets off strang…

MICHAEL: (*As UncleArry.*) Take it you little shit!

MICHELLE: Said UncleArry, slapping the back of my head. But no sooner had I said 'ow' than Mister Bought and Smite clicked his fingers and his gorilla lazily unfolded one huge arm, the fist of which connected with UncleArry's head and sent him flying into an already demolished couch, while the index finger of his other hand pulled out a bogey the size of a baby's head. This he ate.

(*As Mister Bought and Smite.*) Arry you scamp. Forgive him children: he is merely high-spirited. Now. Down to business. Would you like to come with Mr Boughton-Smythe, off to his hise in the country and there to be treated like royalty for the rest of your youths, or would you like to go back to your dingy little council flat to face a life of chips and petty crime? Take your time, no hurry, but tell me now. Do you want to come with me?

Pause.

MICHAEL: He was a stranger.

MICHELLE: He had a gorilla.

MICHAEL: Who had smacked UncleArry clear across the room.

MICHELLE: But he had a big house.

MICHAEL: And such big words.

MICHELLE: And he smelt so…nice!

Pause.

MICHELLE /MICHAEL: (*Together.*) Yes!

MICHELLE: (*As Mister Bought and Smite.*) Ah, and so it is settled. Arry?

MICHAEL: Who was extracting himself from the remains of the couch.

MICHELLE: Have them delivered to me this afternoon. Guy?

MICHAEL steps forward as Guy.

Show Mr Arry how you peel a banana.

He mimes peeling a banana and throwing away the skin.

Show Mr Arry what you do to people who disappoint me.

He does the same mime.

A bargain has been struck, Arry. Do not disappoint me. And with this I take my leave. On Thursday I am dining with Lady Toynbee – do you know her? Of the Shropshire Toynbees – and you simply must come along. But do bathe first. One can take irony only so far.

MICHAEL: And with that he was gone. UncleArry waited for a minute, then leapt into the air and danced around the room rubbing his hands and screamed with laughter.

(*As UncleArry.*) Yes! Yesyesyesyesyes!

(*As himself.*) UncleArry was happy.

MICHELLE: It was good to see UncleArry happy. And then he turned to us.

MICHAEL: Well my little darlings…

MICHELLE: Said UncleArry.

MICHAEL: …you've behaved yourself very well. Very well indeed! UncleArry is pleased, and you're going off to live in the big house.

MICHELLE: Hooray!

MICHAEL: But first…

MICHELLE: Said UncleArry.

MICHAEL: …to show you how pleased I am…

MICHELLE: And he began to move towards us…

MICHAEL: …we're going to play a little game…

MICHELLE: …a strange expression on his face.

MICHAEL: …a little game of…

MICHELLE: We like games.

MICHAEL: …affection.

MICHELLE: This confused us.

MICHAEL: You may as well get used to it now…

MICHELLE: And slowly, UncleArry reached out his hands to us…

Suddenly the door bursts open…

MICHAEL: Smashing my sister in the face…

MICHELLE: …and there in the doorway…

MICHAEL: Angry as thunder…

MICHELLE: Bigger than ever before…

MICHAEL: Vomit still clinging to his ears…

MICHELLE: Dad!

MICHAEL: Shhh! UncleArry drops us as quick as a flash, and begins to back away like a frightened rabbit.

MICHELLE: But before he can bolt our bull of a father – who hasn't yet seen us – steams forward and pins him by his throat to the wall!

MICHAEL: Good ta see ya!

MICHELLE: Squeaks UncleArry.

MICHAEL: I can explain everything.

MICHELLE: You fhacking bastard!

MICHAEL: Bellows Daddy.

MICHELLE: I'll Fhacking 'ave you!

MICHAEL: And pulls back his fist to pound that face into the wall. UncleArry thinks quicker than he's ever done before, and whips out Dad's wallet.

(*As UncleArry.*) Here y'are!

MICHELLE: Says UncleArry.

MICHAEL: No harm done.

MICHELLE: Father, with one hand still to UncleArry's throat, takes the wallet, opens it up and checks the contents. And there we see a little red blinking light.

MICHAEL: Being a careful man – some would say a tight bastard – our father had had his wallet fitted with a tracking device.

MICHELLE: A thoughtful precaution that he somehow never felt necessary to bestow upon his children. He pockets the wallet and looks deep into UncleArry's eyes.

My kids. I want my kids.

MICHAEL: Ah, now leave me the kiddies, eh?

MICHELLE: I want my kids.

MICHAEL: I can pay.

MICHELLE: I want my kids.

MICHAEL: More money than you can drink in a year!

MICHELLE: I want my fhacking kids!

MICHAEL: And can it be?

MICHELLE: We see him there.

MICHAEL: The same Dad he's always been.

MICHELLE: Smelly and drunk.

MICHAEL: Angry and thick.

MICHELLE: Big and stupid.

MICHAEL: But there is a tear in his eye.

MICHELLE: And he is willing – and I swear it's true – to squeeze the life out of another man's neck to get his children back.

They exchange a look. She makes a decision.

Dad!!

MICHAEL: Shhhh!

MICHELLE: Daddy, Daddy!!!

MICHAEL: Shut up!

MICHELLE: Dad, Daddy, Daddy, DAD!

Pause.

MICHAEL: And Daddy turns round and at last notices us – UncleArry sliding to the floor unseen in his own private world of fear – and the tear that was in his eye rolls down his cheek, over his vomit-encrusted lips, and hits the floor with a sound like the world's biggest heartbeat. He looks down at us. He says:

MICHELLE: Every man has his crosses to bear.

MICHAEL: And he turns sadly and heads for the door. He stops there. He seems to be quivering. And over his shoulder he says:

MICHELLE: Come on you little cunts.

MICHAEL: And we follow him out.

MICHELLE: Thinking sadly of peeled bananas.

MICHAEL: Of ice cream and servants.

MICHELLE: Of something called champagne.

MICHAEL: And I know that my tenacious little sister is thinking…

MICHELLE: That you should've squeezed just a little bit harder.

I look at my brother

And something in him has changed.

Something is different.

An awareness.

He is now aware

That there are lives different from ours.

Things won't be the same.

IN THE BEGINNING

MICHAEL: …dragging home this, in my hands, it's heavy, this TV is heavy, I'm dragging home this TV, my mind is light, racing, like an engine out of gear, spinning through, and in my hands this thing is, this thing is heavy, I can feel

my breast heavy, pulsing with blood, aching with blood
and my mind beats with thoughts one after the other,
one thought kicking the other out, throwing the, forcing
the, but soon it's one, just one, just one thought endlessly
replacing itself endlessly as I carry, as I drag, as I heave,
one thought, the thought of my boy, the only thought,
no longer thinking of my dad's, to the telly, his reaction
to what I'm, not of my sister hiding Debris just for those
hours, not of the feeling which emanating from, the feeling
which I hadn't, but just one relentless thought, my boy, my
boy, my boy, my boy, my boy, my boy, my boy, my boy,
my boy, my boy Debris, that's the only thought, so when
I, I go in, when I go in and see, look at, see the face on my
sister, her face has this look and my heart drains of blood,
ice, my body walks into a soft concrete wall, her face, her
look is an expletive from God, a cup of bleach in the eyes,
a full stop, a sound too loud to hear, so I know something
is, I instantly know something is not, I know in that instant
that something is not right. And she is not holding my boy.
She is not holding Debris. I follow her eyes. My dad sits on
the couch cradling Debris in his arms. My father and my
son. And her.

MICHELLE: He came in.

MICHAEL: Panic pounding, breath catching, eyes stinging
what the what the what the what the what the –

MICHELLE: He came in.

MICHAEL: What?

MICHELLE: I was just playing with the boy and he came in, he
just came in.

MICHAEL: Why didn't you lock the –

MICHELLE: I forgot. I must've forgot. I… He hasn't hurt it.
He…it's weird.

MICHAEL: – holding my boy, sitting there, he was just sitting,
he was just sitting there holding my boy and the look, my

sister's face had this look, and I knew, I knew that she had done this – on purpose, I knew that she had done this on purpose...

MICHELLE: He just came in.

MICHAEL: You've done this on purpose.

MICHELLE: He hasn't hurt it.

MICHAEL: – holding my, holding my, holding my –

MICHELLE: It's weird. Look.

MICHAEL: I looked. And then...

MICHELLE: ...the strangest...

MICHAEL: ...thing...

MICHELLE: ...that we had...

MICHAEL: ...ever, in our...

MICHELLE: ...lives seen...

MICHAEL: ...happened. He began to talk to the baby.

MICHELLE: You are so beautiful. Your fingers. Your perfect little fingers. Your little nails.

MICHAEL: He didn't shout. He didn't growl. He didn't scream. He didn't snarl. He talked. We'd never seen him do that. We were transfixed.

MICHELLE: So beautiful. (*To someone who isn't there.*) Beautiful. You've made such a beautiful boy.

He began to talk to someone who wasn't there.

MICHAEL: – holding my, holding my, holding my and my soul freezes, it screams, it becomes solid mercury and shatters into a thousand tiny sharp pieces and the pieces are the only things I my mind, screaming pain into my brain –

MICHELLE: He had to be beautiful, coz you are.

He's talking to my mother.

MICHAEL: – My brain is full of them –

MICHELLE: This is where our lives begin.

MICHAEL: So I go to the phone, the phone, remember? The phone, another phone another house a normal house, but this is a different phone, a phone in the street –

MICHELLE: The hope, the possibility.

MICHAEL: – and I call I call the people who would take because this I cannot have this I cannot watch, this joy, this hope, this hope, this possibility for another I call the people.

MICHELLE: My father and my mother.

MICHAEL: – I call the people –

MICHELLE: In the beginning.

MICHAEL: I call the people who would take my I call the people who would take my boy away.

Long pause.

MICHELLE: In the beginning

There is God,

And he's bored.

He's bored shitless.

He wanders around for an eternity of eternities,

Scratching his balls,

Fuck all to do.

So:

Fourteen billion years ago he makes a bang

And he waits.

Nine billion years and the gases and dirt squish together to form the earth,

And he waits, watching, as a billion years later

Primitive single cell organisms with no nuclei form in a piece of mucus.

Within three hundred million years there are animals and plants in the oceans,

God watching in anticipation as in another couple of hundred million years

The plants develop the courage to try their luck on dry land,

Followed by hungry animals that are scared of being lonely.

He watches happily as sixty five million years ago an asteroid smashes into the earth,

And the dinosaurs realise they're too big and stupid to survive,

And it's around this time that a little thing that looks like a lemur makes its appearance.

Twelve million years ago the lemurs' descendants part company with their friends,

One branch becoming orang-utans, one becoming us,

And time now whizzes past as primates become human,

As they pick up rocks and smash each other over the head,

As they domesticate plants, push out the Neanderthals, learn language and become aware that something is watching.

Wars come and go, slavery, cannibalism, persecution, torture, the invention of the wheel, the invention of the factory,

And eventually this squabbling mass of bipedal fury finally coalesces into my mother and father,

And now God is watching, he's on the edge of his fucking seat, dribbling in anticipation.

He watches their love, their marriage, their fights, their arguments, their first born, the conception and gestation of a little girl, and there we are and there God is on, on that day, that day when my mother complains of pains, terrible pains, and my father, who now knows his life has been denied, my father who sits stunned and drunk in front of the telly watching the life he wants while steeping in the one he hates, ignores her, shouts at her, tells her to fuck herself, she's not due yet, she's got months, it's just wind you fat cunt, and this is the moment, this is the moment and God watches happily as my father refuses, will not, cannot get help, will not believe there's anything –

And suddenly

Her appendix pops.

And she dies.

That was the moment.

That was it.

God sits back.

He rolls a fag.

He grins the satisfaction of a job well done.

He doesn't watch as I am ripped from my mother's corpse on a hospital slab.

He takes little interest in my father's howls.

He doesn't notice my brother scrabbling around alone.

But we know.

We know.

We know that from that moment on God is no longer watching.

Pause.

When they came to take Debris away my father had to be tranquillised with a feather dart before the boy could once more be pried free.

MICHAEL: They found him hiding in someone's garden, a blood red kiss on his cheek from little Debris leaving them in no doubt as to who he was. They say that just before he went under for a second he became absolutely lucid and seemed to be saying sorry to someone who wasn't there.

MICHELLE: When my dad came round he said nothing. He'd given up speaking. But I saw his betrayed eyes following my brother around the flat and hatching a plan to make him see. And we knew –

MICHAEL: – that nothing would be safe from our father's anger.

Every now and then my breast aches and I think of Debris. It's heavy with blood, aching for his lips. And sometimes I fantasize that Babies are not found in rubbish and that somewhere he has a mother whose breast, heavy with milk, throbs in time with mine. I imagine her scared, not of Debris' death, but of his life, placing her boy gently in some warm garbage, unable to cope. I imagine her face. I imagine her tears. I imagine her tears mingling with mine.

MICHELLE /MICHAEL: (*Together.*) I.

Imagine.

Her.

End

OSAMA THE HERO

Characters

GARY
seventeen (m)

FRANCIS
late twenties (m)

LOUISE
mid-twenties (f)

MANDY
fifteen / sixteen (f)

MARK
fifty (m)

Osama The Hero was initially written and developed as part of Paines Plough's Wild Lunch 2004. It was first produced by the Hampstead Theatre on 5 May 2005 with the following cast:

MANDY, Christine Bottomley

GARY, Tom Brooke

FRANCIS, Ian Dunn

MARK, Michael Mears

LOUISE, Rachel Sanders

Director Anthony Clark

Designer Patrick Connellan

Lighting Designer James Farncombe

Sound Designer John Leonard

One

GARY, FRANCIS and LOUISE, MANDY and MARK. GARY talks directly to the audience, FRANCIS and LOUISE to each other, MANDY and MARK to the audience as though talking to camera.

GARY: I'm not stupid.

FRANCIS: Dirty fucking pervert.

LOUISE: Francis –

FRANCIS: Dirty. Fucking. Pervert.

LOUISE: Look, Francis

FRANCIS: Do you like perverts?

LOUISE: No, of course I –

FRANCIS: Do you like dirt?

LOUISE: I don't like dirt.

FRANCIS: Then why are we having this discussion?

GARY: I'm definitely not stupid. People say I am, but that's probably a jealous instinct. If you don't understand something you just become jealous of it. I don't understand myself sometimes. But I'm not jealous of myself.

Sorry, that's confused me.

LOUISE: We have to have this discussion.

FRANCIS: No we don't.

LOUISE: We do.

FRANCIS: We don't.

LOUISE: We do.

FRANCIS: No we don't.

LOUISE: We do, because –

FRANCIS: Why do we?

LOUISE: Because, we do because, I'm telling you why, actually –

FRANCIS: Why do we have to have this discussion?

LOUISE: if you'd listen, listen, if you'd listen Francis, I'm telling you why –

FRANCIS: Well tell me fucking why, then.

LOUISE: I am telling you fucking why, if you'd listen, if you'd please listen I'm telling you fucking why

GARY: I once imagined a world where you could buy a synthetic form of love which was inserted into the anus and you could just buy this, everyone could just buy this and be in love if they wanted and it was a positive, when you think about it it was a positive thing, but then I couldn't remember whether it was something I'd seen on TV and maybe I hadn't imagined it after all. I'm thinking of becoming a terrorist.

LOUISE: We have to have this discussion because you're likely to get yourself into trouble again.

FRANCIS: I'm older than you, Louise, and please don't say things like that, because that's just really fucking stupid.

LOUISE: You're likely to go off.

FRANCIS: You're not Nelson Mandela, Louise

LOUISE: You're likely to get some idea in your head

FRANCIS: Kofi Annan, you're not Kofi Annan, Louise

LOUISE: and someone is likely to get hurt because of your brain.

FRANCIS: And what about you? What about your brain?

LOUISE: What about me?

FRANCIS: Are you going to help me or not?

LOUISE: Are you going to calm down.

FRANCIS: I'm calm, I'm calm, this is calm…

GARY: I watched things on telly, American things, and I'd
    think that's what I wanna do, I wanna be a pathologist, or
    I wanna go skiing and then the programme would end and
    I'd turn and look at my mum and in my heart I knew that
    she was sitting in her own urine again and I'd have to admit

FRANCIS: I'm not going to hurt anyone.

GARY: I'd get a funny feeling

FRANCIS: I'm not going to use violence

GARY: I have to admit that I'd get a funny feeling in the pits of
    my stomach

FRANCIS: I'm not going to be a bad person.

GARY: and then I would feel bad.

FRANCIS: I'm going to kick the fucking shit out of him.

    Pause.

MANDY: and, for us it's not really about the money

MARK: or the fame

MANDY: or the glamour and the

MARK: the cruises

MANDY: the Oscars, the adulation, it's not really about that
    'stuff'

MARK: record contracts

MANDY: it's more about saying

MARK: signings, jets, dinners with religious leaders

MANDY: saying something to people out there

MARK: wealth and glory

MANDY: saying something to ordinary people, just

MARK: because that's what we are, ordinary is

MANDY: that's what we have is an ordinary

MARK: to be honest

MANDY: our appeal

MARK: if that's what we have, if appeal is

MANDY: oh we do

MARK: oh we definitely do, yes, alright

MANDY: we do

MARK: we do have that, that appeal, but the point is

MANDY: the point we'd like to make

MARK: is that we are just ordinary, an ordinary

MANDY: we sit in front of the television and eat

MARK: chips

MANDY: fruit

MARK: fruit, yes, though sometimes, but yes, we sit there with our little boy

MANDY: little Armistice

MARK: we sit there with our little Armistice

MANDY: beautiful little

MARK: beautiful little Armistice, yes, just like any ordinary couple anywhere in any world

MANDY: and the point we'd like to make is that it's easy to look at us and think

MARK: you know

MANDY: look at them

MARK: envy

MANDY: well…

MARK: you know, look at them

MANDY: but we are you

MARK: and that's why we'd like to be a beacon

MANDY: a beacon of hope and dreams that shines out across this world and says

MARK: and says

MANDY: and says it's possible.

MARK: If it's possible for us,

MANDY: If it's possible for us,

MARK: It's possible for you

MANDY: It's possible for you too, to be like us.

Pause.

MARK: Though not all of you.

MANDY: No

MARK: because

MANDY: no, not all of you

MARK: that would not be possible

MANDY: not everyone can be like us

MARK: that wouldn't be right.

MANDY: at all

MARK: And there's nothing wrong with being you.

MANDY: Fuck, no.

MARK: Don't say fuck, darling.

MANDY: Sorry.

MARK: Which is the message we'd like to

MANDY: Sorry about that.

MARK: which is the message we'd like to give.

MANDY: I am sorry.

MARK: It's okay to be yourself but use us as an example. If you want to.

MANDY: Yes.

MARK: Yes.

MANDY: Yes.

Pause.

MARK: Can I touch you?

Beat.

MANDY: You can't say that.

MARK: Sorry. Sorry.

Can I? Can I though? Please?

GARY: I'm the sort of person that likes to think of my weaknesses as my strengths.

I heard someone say that on television once and I thought that's good, I'll have that, that's good.

MARK: Just let me touch your sleeve.

MANDY: No. No touching.

GARY: I see what's going on, I think things through.

MARK: I can't stand this feeling, it's like someone has injected my body with an extra two pints of blood.

MANDY: I'll go.

MARK: Please don't go.

GARY: Bins have been blowing up on our estate this summer and that's not me. Just so you know, just so you know and are aware that that's not me. I'm walking home suddenly there's this pop, like a twenty foot bag of crisps being stood on, millisecond of intense silence, rush of air. Twenty feet away there is a fire in what's left of a bin, which is now nothing but twisting snakes of metal attached to the ground and I'm looking around thinking who's done that and were they deliberately trying to get me and then I notice the first twitch. Second twitch. Third twitch. Spin round, the entire estate, curtains twitching, every window, curtains twitching at me and for a second I see the view from thirty or forty different perspectives, looking down at me, suddenly I'm looking down at me from thirty or forty different perspectives at me twenty feet away from a burning bin and I can feel them all thinking one thought, one thought in all their brain, 'him' they're thinking, 'him'.

FRANCIS: What do you think of an old man inviting a young girl into his garage?

LOUISE: She's not a young girl.

FRANCIS: She's younger than you.

LOUISE: She's younger than you.

GARY: I have a fantasy where I ask a girl out. She says yes. I take her to Heathrow airport and we spend the entire day watching the planes taking off and it's a beautiful day, the sun's shining, she's laughing at my jokes, I think she has blonde hair, but I could be wrong. And what's strange is that when it ends I often feel that an organ in my stomach has disappeared. Funny, eh.

I'm not stupid.

FRANCIS: What do you think of an old man walking out on his wife of twenty-two years?

LOUISE: I think you're getting angry.

FRANCIS: What do you think of an old man walking out on his wife of twenty-two years and inviting an underage girl into his garage? Someone no-one likes.

LOUISE: I like her.

FRANCIS: Not too bright, vulnerable, what do you think of that?

LOUISE: I think you need to get out, get a job, get moving.

FRANCIS: What do you think of that?

LOUISE: sitting in here watching

FRANCIS: What do you think of that?

LOUISE: curtain twitching, it's not healthy, that's –

FRANCIS: WHAT DO YOU THINK OF THAT?

LOUISE: I THINK IT'S BAD!

FRANCIS: Thank you.

Thank you.

LOUISE: But that doesn't mean you have to start losing control.

FRANCIS: that your answer to everything, get a job? money, status, worlds falling to pieces, terrorists and fucking perverts, you've changed, Louise, it's just a office job but you've really changed. You're different.

LOUISE: I'm not different.

FRANCIS: You're gonna leave me.

LOUISE: Francis, –

FRANCIS: I don't care, leave me, I don't –

LOUISE: Francis –

FRANCIS: Please don't leave me, Louise.

LOUISE: I'm not –

FRANCIS: Where's your garage?

Beat.

Have you got a garage, Louise?

MARK: I like your shoes.

MANDY: Don't say shoes, darling.

MARK: Sorry.

GARY: I never know when things are funny, so what I do is I wait until someone else starts laughing and then I join in, quick as I can, hope I haven't got in too late because there's nothing worse than being left out in the cold with a laugh hanging. People laugh a lot nowadays. I think that's fear.

LOUISE: I'm not answering that question.

FRANCIS: It's a simple question, where's your garage, Louise.

LOUISE: I told you, I'm not answering –

FRANCIS: Where's your garage?

LOUISE: I haven't got a garage.

FRANCIS: Where's my garage?

LOUISE: You haven't got a ga–

FRANCIS: I have got a garage. I have got a garage, Louise.

LOUISE: (*Beat.*) It's burnt out.

FRANCIS: Like all the other garages on this estate except for one.

LOUISE: He didn't burn out the –

FRANCIS: I know he didn't burn out the garage

LOUISE: kids or something, he wasn't here when –

FRANCIS: I know he wasn't here when, that's the point, that's the point I'm making, he wasn't here, he's new and yet he's got a garage?

LOUISE: He pays for it!

FRANCIS: You seen his wife wandering around? Wandering around Louise, looking for him, while he's in the fucking garage. Imagine what it's like to realise you lived with a pervert all these years and then they give him the garage...

LOUISE: He pays for it.

FRANCIS: Dollars. That all that matters? Dollars and fucking perverts?

GARY: Examples of weakness that are also a strength; my non-acceptance of the world. I do not accept what I'm told. I do not believe things just because I've been told things. A strength because, because I get to question things and a weakness because it singles me out as different from them. Further back? You want to go further back...?

MANDY: and in the past there has been great media attention on us, on our family

MARK: Little Armistice.

MANDY: beautiful little

MARK: And people want to know

MANDY: They do, they're very curious.

MARK: they want to know how he's doing and is he taking his first steps,

MANDY: teeth come through

MARK: was it a cold or chicken pox, and you know, we can't just ignore people

MANDY: The fan base.

MARK: though we'd like to sometimes...

MANDY: No we wouldn't.

MARK: Well, sometimes

MANDY: Well, we wouldn't because we love our public.

MARK: Yes, of course, but –

MANDY: We love them and we understand so we wouldn't.

MARK: Alright we wouldn't then.

MANDY: But sometimes we do wish that the media would back off.

MARK: Which is all I was saying.

MANDY: No, not really, but yes we do

MARK: we do

MANDY: we do sometimes, don't we

MARK: we do sometimes ask for our privacy

MANDY: And it's good when that's respected.

MARK: And it's bad when it's not.

MANDY: But it's good when it is.

MARK: Because sometimes I just wish I could kiss you.

MANDY: (*Nervous laugh.*) That's a little...

MARK: Without the public, I mean, you know, but sometimes I sit alone and I close my eyes and I imagine what it would be like to brush my lips against her hair, to breath in the air that was once trapped in the fibres of her skin, to take the moisture from her breath deep into my lungs and eat it, digest it, and part of me feels like cutting a piece out of myself.

Beat.

MANDY: But most of the time we're very happy with the media. We think you do a great job.

Beat.

MARK: Yes.

GARY: This one boy comes in wearing trainers, new trainers, really nice trainers, showing off his trainers to the entire class, not a friend but not an enemy so for me that's a friend, they break his legs, getting the trainers, they break his legs didn't have to, misunderstood the complexities of the social structure and his place within it, I remember sitting for an hour looking at my trainers trying to understand the complexities of the social structure and my place within it. No idea. No idea at all. On the way home Mum stopped me in the street and asked me for some spare change. Breath like pickled death. Gave her some, went home, had fish fingers and pop tarts.

FRANCIS: Dad left me that garage.

GARY: Points of view, it's all about points of view; killing two thousand people's not wrong, it just all depends on what two thousand people it is.

Said that in maths, got detention, said it in media studies and I got an A; she thought I was quoting Orson Welles. Said it in games and I was asked to leave the gym. Teacher looked like he might cry. Didn't say it again.

FRANCIS: Dad left me that garage.

LOUISE: I know!

FRANCIS: It's nothing now.

LOUISE: I know.

FRANCIS: Burnt out piece of shit.

LOUISE: I know.

FRANCIS: I hate this place. But it's our place. It's our fucking place, Louise.

Pause.

(*Singing.*) Every breath you take…

LOUISE: Francis…

FRANCIS: (*Singing.*) Every move you make…

LOUISE: Stop it Francis…

FRANCIS: (*Singing.*) Every bond you break, every step you take…

LOUISE: Shut the fuck up.

FRANCIS: I'll be watching you.

LOUISE: SHUT UP.

FRANCIS: That's a beautiful song, Louise. Dad used to sing that. He used to stand there looking down at you and sing that entire song holding my hand, he'd be holding my hand and we'd both be looking at you and he'd sing every single bar of that song to you.

Copy of *Loot* in your bag.

Beat.

LOUISE: Just looking.

FRANCIS: What for?

LOUISE: Computer.

FRANCIS: Yeah?

LOUISE: Yeah.

FRANCIS: Really?

LOUISE: (*Beat.*) Yeah.

FRANCIS: I love you, Louise.

LOUISE: I love you, Francis.

GARY: We do a project on crimes against humanity. I bring in a copy of *Hello* magazine. They're laughing. I don't understand. Did my presentation, celebrities, breast implants, super rich mansions, quite impassioned, I may have spat once or twice, accidentally and at the end of it I finish and I look up and they're all staring at me. Just staring. Silent.

I remember going to Alton Towers with my mum and that was nice, she didn't drink, not one drink for the entire day. Only thing was she kept putting me on the children's rides, fifteen years old and sitting on a pink elephant with a top hat.

Last week I'm standing outside Dixons watching the news through the shop window and I found that even without the sound I knew exactly what to feel because my body had become conditioned to its emotional structure which was embarrassing because I'm always in tears by the end. It was raining. No-one noticed.

Remember when I was eleven going to church, every week, on my own just going in, but I soon stopped. I think I made them uncomfortable. Mediocrity; that's another example of a weakness that's also a strength. I'm fairly average at everything so that means I manage to survive, but it also means I'm fairly average at everything.

MANDY suddenly laughs extravagantly. MARK realises and joins in, slightly unsure. GARY is about to laugh but gets it wrong, misses the moment and remains silent.

MANDY: Well, that's a very interesting question, but let me answer that first by saying that we believe it's important to find a sense of purpose.

MARK: Absolutely

MANDY: Does that answer your question?

MARK: A sense of direction.

MANDY: Maybe?

MARK: Because without a sense of direction

MANDY: sense of purpose

MARK: What have you really got?

MANDY: Your family, yes

MARK: oh, yes, definitely

MANDY: which is more important to us

MARK: family

MANDY: than anything in the world

MARK: little Armistice

MANDY: anything for that boy

MARK: everything, all of it

MANDY: just to save one of his kidneys

MARK: if we needed too, yes everything

MANDY: without a thought

MARK: if it was absolutely necessary

MANDY: without a heartbeat's hesitation

MARK: because you can live on one.

MANDY: (*Beat.*) What?

MARK: one kidney, you can live on one, is all I'm

MANDY: We'd give everything.

MARK: Yes, yes, everything, but you can buy them for

MANDY: We'd give everything.

MARK: Everything, yes, definitely, everything.

FRANCIS: We can sit here in this and fester or we can aspire, Louise.

MARK: She has the most perfect breasts and if only I could touch them you could shoot me in the back of the head and watch my brains spill out of my face and onto the pavement and I wouldn't mind.

I'm in love with you.

MANDY: Cunt.

MARK: Don't say cunt, darling.

MANDY: Fucking cunt.

MARK: Armistice has a beautiful smile…

MANDY: Beautiful – you fucking – beautiful, yes he does have a beautiful smile.

GARY: Find a hero, a living hero, presentation on a contemporary hero, but it has to be someone who's truly heroic, someone who's an inspiration to millions, a determined individual who'll sacrifice wealth, life and happiness for what they believe in and I scrabble around, I try, I try really hard, no-one, nothing, celebrities, politicians, sportspersons, but to be honest there's nothing, there's nothing, there's nothing and suddenly I find one: BANG! Inspiration, lightning bolt, epiphany, perfect sense. I'm standing in front of the class and I read out the title of my project:

'Osama the Hero.'

FRANCIS: Do you want to aspire, Louise?

LOUISE: Yes.

FRANCIS: Is that what you want?

LOUISE: Yes.

FRANCIS: You're a very beautiful woman.

LOUISE: No, I'm not.

FRANCIS: You are.

LOUISE: I'm not.

FRANCIS: No, you're not, but you are. This is what we have, here, each other. This is our life. This is what we know.

LOUISE: Yes.

FRANCIS: Is there a point to trying to change that?

Louise?

LOUISE: No.

FRANCIS: No.

Please don't talk to me about garages. D'you know why he's put a door in the garage?

LOUISE: To get in and out –

FRANCIS: FUCKING HELL, LOUISE, HE CAN GET IN AND OUT THROUGH THE GARAGE DOOR, THE FUCKING BIG DOOR AT THE FRONT, IF THAT'S –

Pause.

He's put a door in that door, the big door, he's put a little door in the big door so he doesn't have to open the big door and no-one can see inside.

MANDY: We like our privacy.

MARK: Yes, of course.

MANDY: It's an important issue.

MARK: As is love.

MANDY: Respect is important.

MARK: But love is more important.

MANDY: Well, respect is –

MARK: just let me touch your shoes, the soles of your fucking shoes, I don't care, just something

MANDY: respect is

MARK: just something

MANDY: respect is

MARK: just something

MANDY: respect is

MARK: just something

GARY: And I'm telling them, I'm telling them, I'm telling them about a boy, as a young man, twenty-two years old rejecting his family's vast personal fortune, three billion dollars and off into the mountains of Afghanistan to fight the communists, but really, not fight in the way our leaders fight, but really fight and get wounded, not fight like a president or a prime minister, sending boys off to slaughter each other while you eat in the best restaurants and go to concerts and think about what you'll spend your money on when you retire, but go out there with a gun and fight yourself, bleeding, injured, I tell them of a quiet man who rarely laughs but often smiles, who lives simply, eats simply, dresses simply, according to those who have met him a man of impeccable manners who is known never to lie, I explain how despite being on the run in one of the world's poorest regions this man is so well loved that no-one has turned him in to claim the fifty million dollar reward, I explain how this man survived a war against the greatest powers on earth with only a few hundred fighters and little resources and then I look up. And I see the faces. Staring at me. They're just staring at me. Worse than before. This time. This time. This time I know I've really done something.

FRANCIS: What your father did for you.

LOUISE: Don't, Francis.

FRANCIS: He went to prison for you.

LOUISE: Please don't.

FRANCIS: Alright, I won't, but he did, he did do that and you know that he did that, he went to prison to keep you safe and you're just going to let a pervert walk around?

LOUISE: Francis –

FRANCIS: Just walk around as if nothing fucking matters? As if we have no morals?

GARY: Sometimes I get visions of the future. Sometimes I can see myself aged forty, bald, fat, and drunk, thinking of me aged seventeen and the me aged forty is crying and the me aged seventeen is laughing and my head begins to hurt because I'm not sure which one's real.

FRANCIS: If you think I'm going to let that happen you've got another think coming.

MARK: One touch, one touch, of your ear, your arm, the back of your hand, what can it mean to you? it means everything to me; I'm a fifty year-old man and look what you're doing to me.

MANDY: and as long as people can look at us

MARK: I'm grovelling, you've got me grovelling

MANDY: as long as people can look at us and feel

MARK: grovelling in my own shit

MANDY: like they know us and feel secure

MARK: I feel like I've fallen asleep and woken up in my own sick

MANDY: darling, as long they see the family unit

MARK: your hair or your, or your finger or your cheek, I could touch your cheek

MANDY: us with Armistice

MARK: I could touch your chair or your chin or

MANDY: That beautiful boy

MARK: or

MANDY: Alright!

Beat.

MARK: What?

MANDY: One touch.

MARK: Really?

MANDY: One. Just one.

*Beat. Very slowly he reaches out his hand. He cups her breast.
She stands it as long as she can and then pushes his hand away.
He stares at her, hurt, and continues to do so.*

GARY: Bins blow up, more bins and always near me and
you can feel them thinking. I consider being a priest, a
lighthouse keeper, a policeman, a taxidermist, a soldier, a
tramp, an undertaker, a dancer in a gay bar, a footballer, a
tube driver, a drug dealer, a surfer, an accountant, a carer
for a person of disability, a lorry driver and a Buddhist,
but I find myself wondering how much it costs to get to
Afghanistan because maybe then

FRANCIS: This is our place.

GARY: maybe then

FRANCIS: We live here

GARY: maybe then

FRANCIS: We've always lived here

GARY: maybe then

FRANCIS: We always will live here.

Won't we.

LOUISE: Yes.

GARY: maybe then I'd have something to believe in.

MARK: (*Looking back to the audience.*) which of course was how
we felt when little Armistice died.

Beat.

MANDY: What?

MARK: Little Armistice

MANDY: Little…

MARK: yes, little Armistice, little Armistice darling, who died of only one kidney

MANDY: little Armistice isn't

MARK: yes, yes he is darling, he's dead

MANDY: dead?

MARK: poor little dead Armistice

MANDY: no, that's not

MARK: dead, yes, dead, and we cried so hard because he fought so hard, brave little, but he only had his one little kidney

MANDY: One…

MARK: one lonely little kidney, couldn't survive

MANDY: his

MARK: poor little dead Armistice who died of loneliness and neglect

MANDY: no…

MARK: Yes. Yes he did.

And we would like to thank everyone

MANDY: everyone

MARK: everyone, the public, for their support

MANDY: everyone

(*Almost crying.*) everyone for their support.

She gets up and leaves.

MARK: M –?

Mandy

GARY: because word has got around and I can feel…

I can feel the hate.

Oh dear.

FRANCIS: I'm going

to fucking

kill someone

There is a massive explosion.

Two

Inside the now burnt out and blown up garage. GARY sits on a charred chair, hands tied behind his back, gaffer tape over his mouth. FRANCIS stands, staring at him. Walks around him, behind him. Pulls out a single white-bread sandwich in clingfilm. Eats it, thinking. Folds up the clingfilm and puts it back in his pocket. Sits around in front of GARY on a box. Stares at him. Somehow, through his fear, GARY manages to feel embarrassed and looks away.

FRANCIS: D'you know who I am?

No answer.

Oi.

Oi.

Oi, you.

S'alright, I'm just asking you a question.

GARY looks at him.

D'you know who I am?

GARY shakes his head.

Seriously, d'you know who I am?

GARY shakes his head.

Seriously, d'you know who I am? Have you heard of me?

GARY shakes his head.

Look this isn't –

I'm not gonna –

I'm just asking if you've heard of me, that's all.

GARY shakes his head.

Don't shake your head coz that's just winding me up.

GARY doesn't know what to do.

I'm just asking if you've heard of me.

Now, don't give me the answer you think I want, because the answer you think I want is not the answer I want. Okay? It's not a test, I'm not gonna hurt you, it's not loaded, I'm just asking you a simple question d'you know who I am.

Do you know who I am?

GARY doesn't know what to do. Eventually he shakes his head.

What you mean, you don't know who I am? How do you not know who I am? So you've got no idea?

GARY shakes his –

Don't shake your head.

So you've got no idea who I am?

Beat.

No-one ever said anything to you about me?

Beat.

I know who you are, a piece of shit like you, I know all about you and your little presentation, yes, that's right, we know all about that. We have ears, Gary. And you're saying you haven't even got a fucking clue who I am, like no-one on this estate has ever said a word to you about me, ever?

Pause. GARY nods.

So no-one on this estate ever talks about me, no-one ever –

Beat.

You see what happens when you give the answers to questions that you think people want? You get it wrong. You get it wrong, Gary. Honesty is always the best policy.

Pause.

D'you know who my dad was?

Pause. GARY nods.

Whose dad, Gary? Whose fucking dad?

No answer.

I'm gonna tell you a story about my dad. This one
time I brought home a dog, scruffy little mongrel, half
staf, my dad never trusted stafs, I'm about eight, never
ever trusted stafs, found him up the field, brought him
home and my dad says – that's a staf: that's a staf, that'll
turn – but I begged and begged to keep that dog and he
says – alright – because he loved me, Gary – alright, you
can keep that dog but if anything happens – and he didn't
finish his sentence, just if anything happens and that's it.
Week later that dog tears into my sister, tears into her, you
can still see the scar, you ask her, in here on her upper
arm, you ask her, blood…blood…takes her up the hospital,
carries her up the hospital, and I'm at home, hours going
by, fucking shitting, dog as well, both shitting it. He comes
home, says nothing. Gets the dog, gets me, gets a knife.
Goes upstairs. Into the bathroom. Dog in the bath, shaking.
Takes my hand, puts it on the dog's jugular, says – feel that
pulse? – puts the knife into my other hand. Blood hit the
fucking ceiling. Took me forty-five minutes to cut the head
off. Another hour to cut the legs off, through the bone. Put
it in a binbag, took it up the field, chucked it in the lake.
My dad loved me. He loved my sister. D'you understand
that? Gary? Do you understand?

GARY nods.

I'm my father's son.

Don't ever doubt me. Don't ever doubt my ability.

LOUISE enters with MARK. Pause.

MARK: Jesus.

Beat.

Jesus.

FRANCIS: What?

MARK: No, I mean –

FRANCIS: What?

LOUISE: Have you been talking to him?

MARK: No, I don't mean –

FRANCIS: You don't mean what?

MARK: Nothing.

LOUISE: I told you not to talk to him.

FRANCIS: I haven't said…

You're not in charge, Louise, you don't tell me –

LOUISE: I told you to watch him.

FRANCIS: Louise, you're not the boss.

MARK: Jesus fucking Christ.

FRANCIS: Yes, Jesus fucking Christ, and what do you mean you don't mean nothing?

MARK: Sorry?

FRANCIS: You said you don't mean nothing which means you mean something.

MARK: What?

FRANCIS: I'm asking you a question.

MARK: I'm just saying.

FRANCIS: What?

MARK: Fuck.

Jesus.

Beat.

No, good. Good though. No, I mean good though.

FRANCIS: This is him.

MARK: Yes.

FRANCIS: You see?

MARK: Yes.

FRANCIS: I got him.

LOUISE: We got him.

FRANCIS: We got, yeah, we got him.

LOUISE: His hands are hurting.

FRANCIS: Not the police, Mark; us, me and my sister.

LOUISE: Ropes are too tight.

MARK: This is the one?

FRANCIS: This is the one, this is the one.

LOUISE: Look like they're gonna bleed.

MARK: So what are we gonna do?

LOUISE: I said let them fucking well bleed.

Beat.

FRANCIS: What?

MARK: What are we going to, you know.

FRANCIS: Are you taking the piss?

MARK: I'm just asking.

FRANCIS: The police are doing nothing, Mark.

MARK: I know, I'm just asking because –

FRANCIS: I thought you said you wanted to be involved.

MARK: I do, I do wanna be –

FRANCIS: I thought you said you was interested.

LOUISE: We got him.

MARK: No, no it's just a question, I'm just, I'm just –

FRANCIS: Are you not interested?

LOUISE: Of course he's interested.

FRANCIS: Are you not bothered?

MARK: Of course I'm bothered.

FRANCIS: Because if you're not bothered or interested about things around here…

MARK: I said good

FRANCIS: This was the last garage on the estate, Mark, you had the last garage on the estate and now it's been blown up, what sort of people are we if we allow this to happen?

MARK: I said good, didn't I say –

Louise, didn't I say, the first thing I said was good.

Beat.

LOUISE: You can still smell what he did here.

MARK: I know.

LOUISE: To you, Mark. This is your garage

FRANCIS: Your fucking garage, Mark.

MARK: Yeah, I know.

LOUISE: Can still see the blood, he blew up your garage.

MARK: We know that?

FRANCIS: Exactly.

MARK: No, I'm asking.

FRANCIS: What?

MARK: I'm asking if we, you know.

FRANCIS: What's the matter with you? We know.

MARK: Okay.

FRANCIS: You know, you fucking know.

MARK: Yes.

FRANCIS: We live here, we know, do you live here?

MARK: Yes, I live here

FRANCIS: Then you know, don't you know?

MARK: I know, yes I…

Little…sod.

FRANCIS: Yes, yes, little prick, little cunt, little fucking cunt.

We've been here longer than you, Mark.

MARK: What's that got to do with –

FRANCIS: I'm just saying we've been here longer than you.

LOUISE: Don't start with that, Francis.

FRANCIS: We've been here longer.

LOUISE: I thought we agreed to leave that –

MARK: We agreed to leave that –

LOUISE: I thought –

FRANCIS: I'm not attacking him, I'm just saying.

LOUISE: Calm down, Francis.

FRANCIS: You calm down.

MARK: We're standing here in a burnt out garage with a tied up boy.

LOUISE: Your burnt out garage.

    Your burnt out garage, Mark.

MARK: We know it's him?

FRANCIS: Of course we know it's him.

MARK: How do we know it's him.

LOUISE: We know what he's been saying.

FRANCIS: presentations

LOUISE: We know what sort of person he is

FRANCIS: explosions, bins, presen-fucking-tations, Gary

MARK: Because if it wasn't

LOUISE: It was him.

    Beat.

MARK: We should talk to him.

FRANCIS: Oh we're going to talk to him.

LOUISE: That's what I said.

FRANCIS: We're going to talk to him alright.

LOUISE: I said we should talk to him.

FRANCIS: Louise, please don't do that.

LOUISE: What?

FRANCIS: Try and make me look small.

MARK: His hands are hurting.

LOUISE: Fuck his hands.

MARK: His wrists are bleeding.

LOUISE: Fuck his wrists.

FRANCIS: And stop swearing so much.

LOUISE: (*To MARK.*) Where's your wife?

No answer.

Where's your wife?

No answer.

(*To GARY.*) Do you know where his wife is?

MARK: She's in hospital.

LOUISE: You put her in hospital. He put her in hospital.

FRANCIS: Doesn't that make you feel anything?

MARK: Of course it does.

FRANCIS: For fuck's sake.

MARK: I'm saying it does.

FRANCIS: People like us, walking around, in danger, my sister in danger, we shouldn't be walking around in –

MARK: She's doing a bit better.

She's –

Beat.

No, I'm just saying, she's doing a bit better, she's off the drip and –

LOUISE: Mark, whose side are you on?

MARK: Yours, I'm –

LOUISE: Because things have changed.

FRANCIS: Yes.

LOUISE: You have to pick a side. You cannot walk around saying and doing certain things, we cannot let people walk around saying and doing certain things and he has been saying and doing certain things.

FRANCIS: Fucking bastard.

LOUISE: Read the papers. I've got a gas mask.

FRANCIS: She has.

LOUISE: I'm getting ready.

MARK: I know, but –

FRANCIS: Ninety-three year-old woman raped last week.

LOUISE: That's got nothing to do with –

FRANCIS: I know, I'm just saying.

LOUISE: Yeah but don't say.

FRANCIS: Two blocks down. Broke in, stole sixteen pounds fifty, raped her and left. Ruptured her bowel.

LOUISE: Francis, it's nothing to do with that.

FRANCIS: I know, I'm just –

LOUISE: What? You're just what, what are you just doing?

FRANCIS: What about him? Don't shout at me, Louise, what about him? His wife was looking for him.

MARK: What?

FRANCIS: She was looking for you.

MARK: Hey –

FRANCIS: And where were you?

MARK: Yes, I know –

FRANCIS: You were out chasing

MARK: Don't start with all that.

LOUISE: You were nearly in here, Mark.

MARK: I know, I know

LOUISE: Nearly blown to –

MARK: Yes, I know

LOUISE: Lucky escape

FRANCIS: Wife wasn't so lucky.

MARK: Don't bring my wife

LOUISE: We have to bring your wife

FRANCIS: Looking for you

MARK: Don't start with that

FRANCIS: crying her eyes out looking for you and you with a girl

MARK: Hey!

FRANCIS: chasing some child

MARK: Don't start with all the – Louise, don't let him start with the

LOUISE: Shut up, Francis.

FRANCIS: Don't tell me to shut up.

MARK: It's him we should be

FRANCIS: You keep doing this, Louise!

MARK: He did it, he's the one who hurt me, I'm hurt, I'm the, it's me that's hurt!

FRANCIS: Which is what were saying to you Mark!

MARK: Which is what I'm saying, it's me that

FRANCIS: I thought you wanted to do something?

MARK: I do want to do something.

FRANCIS: I thought you we're sick of this shit.

MARK: I am sick of this shit. I am sick of this shit and I do want to do something, just don't bring that into this, because that's my feelings and that has nothing to do with, that's not this.

LOUISE: I heard her crying when they put her in the ambulance. You'd expect her to be screaming or moaning, but she was just crying like a little girl.

FRANCIS: Alright.

MARK: And don't say child.

Pause.

FRANCIS: Show him your scar.

LOUISE: What?

FRANCIS: Show him your scar.

LOUISE: Why?

FRANCIS: Just do it.

LOUISE: No.

FRANCIS: Louise, show him your –

LOUISE: No, why?

FRANCIS: Louise, show him your scar.

LOUISE: Why?

FRANCIS: Because I want to prove a point.

LOUISE: What –

FRANCIS: Louise, please.

Beat.

Please show him your scar.

Pause. She shows MARK her scar.

Not him, him.

LOUISE: You didn't say.

She shows GARY her scar.

FRANCIS: That's who you're dealing with.

LOUISE rolls her sleeve back down. Pause.

So what do we do now?

MARK: We should ask him something.

Make sure.

FRANCIS: What?

MARK: I want to hear him say he did it.

Fair...trial.

FRANCIS: Fair trial?

MARK: Because we should make sure.

FRANCIS: Fair...? He's a fucking terrorist, Mark!

MARK: I want to hear him say it.

LOUISE: We know he did it.

FRANCIS: Yeah, we know he did it.

LOUISE: We should hear him say it, though.

FRANCIS: No, Louise –

LOUISE: Prove he did it.

FRANCIS: No.

LOUISE: Show we're not like him

FRANCIS: No.

LOUISE: Show we're not animals.

FRANCIS: No.

Beat.

MARK: Alright, take the tape off.

FRANCIS: No way.

Beat.

No way.

MARK: You have to take –

FRANCIS: No –

MARK: There's no point if you don't –

FRANCIS: No way, no fucking way.

LOUISE: There's no point if you don't –

FRANCIS: Shut up, Louise, you're supposed to be on my side.

MARK: He can't answer.

FRANCIS: You're my sister.

LOUISE: Take it off.

FRANCIS: No, he'll…he'll scream.

MARK: No-one gives a shit about him.

FRANCIS: No way, you can't take the tape off, that's one thing I know you do not do.

MARK: How's he gonna answer?

FRANCIS: He can nod.

LOUISE: He needs to do more than nod.

FRANCIS: Dad wouldn't take the tape off.

LOUISE: Dad would definitely take the tape off.

FRANCIS: Whose side are you on?

LOUISE: Yours.

FRANCIS: What if he starts screaming? This is not a sane world. Terrorists, rapists, perverts all walking the fucking street and we are the ones who'll get done for this. Don't take the tape off, Louise.

Pause.

MARK: Threaten him.

FRANCIS: What?

MARK: Threaten him.

MARK starts looking through the debris.

FRANCIS: What are you looking for?

MARK finds a slightly charred ball-pin hammer.

MARK: Threaten him with this.

FRANCIS: What?

MARK: Listen, Gary, we're going to take the tape off...

FRANCIS: No –

MARK: We're going to take the tape off and ask you some questions, alright.

Alright?

GARY nods.

And if you scream, I'm...

I'm gonna tap you in the face with this hammer.

Understand?

Beat. GARY nods.

Okay.

(*To FRANCIS.*) Go on.

FRANCIS doesn't move.

Go on.

FRANCIS: Louise –

LOUISE: Go on, Francis.

Beat. FRANCIS goes to GARY.

FRANCIS: If he starts any shit you smack him in the face.

MARK: I will.

FRANCIS: And if he says things that aren't, you know, or against us or something, stupid, you smack him in the face with that hammer.

MARK: I will, I will.

Pause. FRANCIS pulls the tape off.

GARY: Can I go home, please?

MANDY appears, suddenly. FRANCIS puts the tape back on GARY. They stare at MANDY.

MANDY: What?

Beat.

FRANCIS: What the fuck is she doing here?

MARK: Mandy?

FRANCIS: Did you bring her here?

MARK: No.

FRANCIS: This isn't a party!

MARK: I said no.

LOUISE: 'Lo Mandy.

MANDY: Louise.

What you doing with that hammer?

MARK: Just…

Holding it.

FRANCIS: What are you doing here?

MANDY: What are you doing here?

FRANCIS: None of your business.

MARK: Mandy –

MANDY: I know him.

MARK: What are you doing here?

FRANCIS: You forget him.

MARK: Did...did you follow me?

MANDY: No.

FRANCIS: I can't believe –

MARK: Have you been watching me?

MANDY: No.

MARK: I'm not angry, I mean I'd be very –

I've missed you.

MANDY shrugs.

Why haven't you called?

MANDY: Dunno.

MARK: How are you?

MANDY: Alright.

MARK: How's...

Everything?

Your dad?

MANDY: Still a cunt.

FRANCIS: What the fuck are you doing here?

MARK: Don't talk to her like that.

MANDY: He goes to my school.

FRANCIS: Forget him, what the fuck is she doing here?

MARK: She followed me.

MANDY: Didn't follow you.

MARK: It's alright, Mandy, I mean, it's good, if you've been watching –

MANDY: I haven't been watching.

MARK: I missed you.

FRANCIS: Don't you fucking start.

MARK: You could've called.

MANDY: What for?

MARK: To talk to me.

MANDY: Goes to my school.

FRANCIS: You forget you've seen him.

MARK: How've you been?

FRANCIS: Go home. What are you doing here? Did you bring her here?

MARK: I told you –

LOUISE: Gary blew up the garage, Mandy.

MANDY: How d'you know that?

LOUISE: He's said certain things that point solidly in that direction.

So we're defending ourselves.

Beat.

MANDY: He's a freak.

LOUISE: What are you doing here?

MANDY: Just come here sometimes. Used to like it here.

MARK: With me.

MANDY: Used to like it here. I come here sometimes. Get out.

Can I stay?

FRANCIS: No.

MANDY: Louise, can I –

MARK: She can –

FRANCIS: No.

MANDY: Don't wanna go home.

FRANCIS: You can't stay.

MANDY: Hate it. Just wanna stay here.

MARK: Let her stay, you can stay –

FRANCIS: No!

MANDY: I'm not his friend. He's a freak. I fucking hate him. He's got no friends. People like me don't mix with people like him, Louise. I've got loads of friends.

FRANCIS: Why don't you go and see them now, then?

MANDY: What, like you go and see yours, you mean?

FRANCIS: Don't start with me, you don't know anything about me.

MANDY: Know enough.

FRANCIS: Get home and keep this buttoned or –

MARK: Don't threaten her.

FRANCIS: What?

MARK: I'm just saying.

FRANCIS: Or what?

MANDY: I know loads of people. Not like him. He has to sit on his own at breaks.

FRANCIS: Or fucking what?

MARK: Look, there's no point in being contrary.

MANDY: On the bus.

FRANCIS: *Contrary*?

MANDY: I'm not like him, Louise. He's shit.

FRANCIS: Contrary?

MANDY: I think he might be mental.

MARK: I don't think this is the time –

FRANCIS: Who's being fucking contrary?

MANDY: Says funny things.

LOUISE: What things?

MARK: Don't start this isn't the time

LOUISE: What things?

MANDY: Said a load of stuff about God last week.

LOUISE: What did he say?

MANDY: (*Beat.*) Stuff.

MARK: She's a young girl, is all I'm –

FRANCIS: Yes, exactly, exactly, Mark, she's a young girl.

MARK: I know, I'm not denying –

LOUISE: What stuff?

MANDY: No God or something.

FRANCIS: You can't deny.

MANDY: That's what's wrong with us.

LOUISE: What's wrong with us?

MARK: I'm not denying that she's young, or that –

FRANCIS: Or that you're a pervert.

MARK: Hey!

MANDY: Said we're all going to die because we haven't got souls or God, or something.

LOUISE: He said that?

MANDY: Something like that.

MARK: Hey, now!

FRANCIS: Chasing some –

LOUISE: She can stay.

FRANCIS: What?

LOUISE: She can stay.

MANDY: Yes!

FRANCIS: Louise!

LOUISE: Let her stay.

FRANCIS: This isn't a game.

LOUISE: Let her stay.

FRANCIS: Yeah, but you're just –

You can't do that, you're just –

LOUISE takes the tape off.

Louise!

GARY: Can I go home now?

LOUISE: No.

FRANCIS: Louise, you can't just…do that.

LOUISE: We wanna ask you some questions.

GARY: I didn't do it.

LOUISE: Do what?

FRANCIS: He's lying.

GARY: Blow this garage up.

FRANCIS: Look, he's lying.

MANDY: Hello, Gary.

LOUISE: Who did it then?

FRANCIS: He doesn't know.

LOUISE: What do you mean, he doesn't know?

FRANCIS: He doesn't know who did it.

LOUISE: Of course he knows. He did it.

FRANCIS: What?

LOUISE: He did it, Francis, of course he fucking knows.

GARY: I didn't do it.

    Beat.

FRANCIS: Yeah, yeah, that's what I mean, I mean, he knows, he did it.

GARY: I don't know.

FRANCIS: You're a dirty fucking liar, Gary, hit him in the face with that hammer.

MANDY: Hello, Gary.

FRANCIS: Just put the tape back on, Louise.

LOUISE: We're asking him questions.

GARY: I didn't do it, I honestly didn't do it.

LOUISE: We think you did.

GARY: Why? I don't understand.

MARK: Why did you blow up my garage?

GARY: I didn't blow up your garage, honestly.

FRANCIS: He's just lying.

MANDY: Aren't you gonna say hello, Gary?

GARY: Alright, Mand.

MARK: Don't talk to her, talk to us.

GARY: She said –

LOUISE: What did you say to her?

GARY: Just said hello.

LOUISE: Before, what did you say before, last week?

GARY: Don't remember.

LOUISE: Yes you do.

FRANCIS: Hit him in the face with the hammer.

GARY: I don't –

LOUISE: About God and we're all gonna die?

FRANCIS: He's giving us shit, hit him in the face.

LOUISE: What was that you said?

MARK: What does it matter?

LOUISE: It matters, what did you say?

FRANCIS: Go on.

GARY: I don't remember.

LOUISE takes the hammer from MARK and hits GARY in the face. He reels back in pain but is silent.

FRANCIS: Fucking hell, Louise, what did you do that for?

LOUISE: You said!

FRANCIS: Yeah, but, fucking – !

LOUISE: What did you say?

GARY doesn't answer. She hits him again.

FRANCIS: Louise! You're hurting him!

LOUISE: What did you say?

GARY: we have to believe in something because if we don't believe in something how can we believe in the future and if we don't believe in the future how can we have a future, not God not Allah not lightning or maybe or maybe me, us or something, forward, a forward, the Egyptians were around for two thousand years it can't be just this, things and, around us, and if you believe in God that's okay but if you believe in the Devil that's the problem because then you can believe others are evil and you want to hurt but maybe there's no good and evil just mistakes and not mistakes.

Pause.

FRANCIS: What the fuck was that?

LOUISE: Was that what he said?

MANDY: Something like that.

FRANCIS: What was all that about?

MARK: Did he blow up my garage?

LOUISE: Did you blow up Mark's garage, Gary?

GARY: No.

FRANCIS: What the fuck are you on, Gary?

LOUISE: Are you a terrorist, Gary?

GARY: No, I am not a terrorist, Louise.

LOUISE: Don't use my name, why've you been saying these things?

GARY: Dunno, they're just things.

LOUISE: Do you hate us?

GARY: No.

LOUISE: Do you despise us?

GARY: No, I don't.

MANDY: He does.

FRANCIS: He doesn't, he looks up to us, someone like him.

MANDY: You don't now him.

FRANCIS: Who the fuck invited you here?

LOUISE: Did you see Mark's wife?

GARY: No.

MARK: No-one invited her, she followed me.

LOUISE: There was part of a carrier bag stuck to her face.

MANDY: Didn't follow you.

LOUISE: Tesco's bag, only the heat had shrunk it, like you used to do with crisp packets, putting them under the grill.

MARK: No, but you came back to be here.

MANDY: So?

LOUISE: You could still see the name, but really small, it was shrunk really small.

MARK: Thinking of me, thinking of us.

MANDY: No!

LOUISE: Just as they lifted her into the ambulance it fell off.

MANDY: Thinking of here, not you.

MARK: We can still –

MANDY: Not you, thinking of being here, thinking of being

MARK: we can –

MANDY: someone else.

LOUISE: Just lazily drifted off. Took her skin off. All down the side of her face. Eye socket to lip.

MANDY: You're just creepy.

MARK: Mandy –

LOUISE: Just lazily peeled off her face. Could see the eye-ball sitting into the bone.

MANDY: This is all gone. Dirty old creep. Like sick.

MARK: Mandy –

MANDY: All. Gone.

Okay?

Beat.

LOUISE: Meat and bone. It was like looking at a living face of meat and bone.

Beat.

Tell us why you did it?

GARY: I didn't do it.

LOUISE: Mark, hold this.

Tell us why you did it.

GARY: I can't because I didn't do it.

FRANCIS: He don't look well.

LOUISE: Mark?

MARK takes the hammer.

GARY: Honestly, I didn't.

FRANCIS: Maybe he's had enough.

MARK: Little…sod.

GARY: I didn't –

MARK: Little prick.

GARY: Honestly.

MARK: Little cunt, little fucking cunt.

LOUISE: Tell us how you did it then, little cunt.

GARY: What?

MARK: This is my home.

GARY: How can I tell you how when I didn't do it?

LOUISE: Gary, we're not going to hurt you if you tell us.

GARY: Really?

LOUISE: Yes.

MARK: My wife, my fucking wife!

GARY: But...

LOUISE: What?

MARK: This is where I live, in my own home!

GARY: But...

LOUISE: But what, Gary.

GARY: But I didn't do it.

MARK: Don't say you didn't do it.

GARY: But I didn't –

MARK: DON'T SAY YOU DIDN'T DO IT!

LOUISE: Gary?

GARY: What makes you think I did it?

FRANCIS: Those ropes are hurting him, you see.

MANDY: We know you did it.

GARY: You don't, you don't know, you need evidence or –

LOUISE: You don't need evidence.

MARK: Stop pissing around.

LOUISE: You don't need evidence for terrorists.

If you say you did it we'll let you go.

GARY: Will you?

LOUISE: Yes.

Pause. GARY looks at them. Looks at FRANCIS.

GARY: But I didn't.

Beat.

LOUISE: Lie the chair down.

They look at her.

Lie the chair down, back against the floor.

MARK lies the chair down, GARY's head upstage.

FRANCIS: Watch his hands, Louise watch his –

MARK and LOUISE kneel at his head.

MARK: Twenty-two years of marriage, twenty-fucking-two years!

LOUISE: Put the tape on him, Mandy.

Mandy?

GARY: Honesty's the best –

MANDY puts the tape back on.

LOUISE: Gary? I want you to nod that you did it. If you don't Mark's going to smash you in the teeth with his hammer. D'you understand?

GARY nods.

FRANCIS: Louise –

LOUISE: Make sure his skull's against the floor.

FRANCIS: Maybe he's had enough.

MARK: Filthy little

LOUISE: Did you do it?

MARK: pervert,

MANDY: He's really scared.

MARK: filthy pervert

FRANCIS: Louise?

LOUISE: Gary, did you do it?

Shakes his head.

Hit him.

MARK smashes the ball of the hammer into the front of his mouth.
MANDY looks away.

FRANCIS: Fuck!

MARK: Pervert.

LOUISE: Gary, did you do it?

Gary?

GARY shakes his head.

Hit him.

FRANCIS: Don't hit him!

MARK hits his teeth again.

MARK: dirty

FRANCIS: Stop!

MANDY: God.

FRANCIS: Louise, stop, please, he's –

LOUISE: He's a terrorist.

FRANCIS: He's –

LOUISE: Don't be weak.

FRANCIS: I'm not weak.

LOUISE: Did you do it?

GARY shakes his head. MARK hits him in the mouth again, choosing a different angle to get at teeth that haven't been smashed.

MARK: filthy

FRANCIS: He's had enough!

LOUISE: Hit him.

Again, a different angle.

MARK: fucking

MANDY: God.

LOUISE: Hit him.

Again, a different angle.

MARK: pervert.

Pause. FRANCIS is crying now, away from them, cannot watch. MANDY is unable to take her eyes from GARY's mouth. LOUISE takes the hammer from MARK. MARK sits back. GARY is still silent.

Oh dear.

MANDY: Jesus.

MARK: Oh dear, then.

MANDY: He's choking.

LOUISE: What?

MANDY: He's choking on the blood.

LOUISE: Then…take the tape off.

MARK: Oh dear, then.

MANDY begins to take the tape off.

MANDY: Jesus.

MARK: Oh dear.

MANDY: His lip's stuck…it's hanging, it's…

LOUISE: Just pull it.

She pulls. Rips his lip off.

MANDY: Jesus Christ!

LOUISE: It's alright. This is…

Beat.

Won't do his…

Now, won't do his…

It's alright –

FRANCIS: It's not fucking alright!

LOUISE: won't do his

presentations

again. Eh?

No, it's alright, we were…

We were…

MANDY: His teeth…

LOUISE: it's alright.

MANDY: His teeth are all…

LOUISE: It's alright.

MANDY: I think a piece of his gum's missing…

MARK: Oh dear, then.

LOUISE: No, it's, it's alright. It is, it's

MANDY: Where, has he swallowed it?

LOUISE: It's alright.

MANDY: Jesus.

FRANCIS: Shit, shit.

LOUISE: It's alright. It's alright, Mandy. It's alright, Francis.

MARK: Oh dear.

Oh dear, then.

Oh dear.

Beat.

Well that's…

That's

LOUISE: Francis?

MANDY: Louise?

MARK: That's

MANDY: Louise?

MARK: that. Then.

Pause.

LOUISE: They moved a paedophile to this estate. My dad
waited for him. Smashed his feet with a baseball bat. He
did that for me. I was fourteen. He went to prison. Died
in there of stomach cancer. That paedophile walks around
today.

MANDY: Louise?

LOUISE: I love you, Francis.

No answer.

Gary's an agent of terror.

MANDY: Louise?

LOUISE: Francis, I love you.

MANDY: Louise?

LOUISE: We did a good thing here today.

We did...

We did a good thing.

MANDY: Louise?

Three

MANDY, MARK, FRANCIS, LOUISE, isolated from each other.

MARK: So I'm standing there cooking this Salmon Teriyaki –
which is a lot easier than it looks, it's actually a really easy
dish, I mean really, the trick is to get the right rice, you get
the right rice and the whole thing, you get this Japanese
rice, that's the key, you have to get this Japanese rice, but
you can get this in supermarkets these days, it's rounder,
this rice, Tesco's or, they use it in Sushi, or Sainsbury's
probably and the shape is, I think the texture is, you know
the difference immediately, rounder maybe a bit sweeter,
I'm not sure, but you get this rice and what I do is I have
these bowls and once it's cooked I pack the rice into these
bowls, tip it onto the plate, give it a twist then take the
bowl away, and because this rice is sticky you have this
dome, this little dome of rice, it's really very easy but it
looks, you know, it looks, and then it's just salmon steaks
which I fry in the pan in a little olive oil and sprinkle a bit
of flour, this isn't rocket science I know, but I sprinkle a
bit of flour before putting it in the pan because it takes the
moisture from the flesh which crisps up the skin, I know,
I know, I fucking know, that's no revelation, I mean this
isn't, it's a very easy thing and it's cook the salmon and at
the last minute it's in with the Teriyaki – which comes in a
bottle and usually I feel, a bottle, you know, some celebrity
chef's sauce in a bottle, it feels like cheating, usually, but
this is, and you can do better than this cunt yourself, but
this is, it comes in a bottle that's how Teriyaki comes, it's
like soy sauce, this is how it comes, so at the last minute
you splash in the Teriyaki into the hot pan, just for a
minute, and then serve, salmon next to the rice, which is
in a dome and drizzle the fish with the sauce and a little
on the rice, which doesn't break apart because it's a sticky
rice, it looks fantastic, and maybe a hint of green, spinach
or, or, I do these beans, Japanese style green beans, but
that's not important, it always looks fantastic but, it's really

a very easy thing to cook and I'm standing there cooking, and I say cooking but I mean watching, because honestly this is so fucking easy, and I'm standing there cooking this Salmon Teriyaki and I hear the door open and I know she's home. And she comes into the kitchen. Not a word. I carry on watching my Salmon Teriyaki. Hitting the meat of the fish with my spatula, no reason, just, you know. She puts something down; bags; shopping-bag, the sound of apples hitting the table through the plastic of the carrier-bag: keys on the table. And then she's behind me. Peering over my shoulder. And this is a big gesture – much bigger than it looks because she always used to come up behind me and rest her chin on my shoulder and watch me cooking and though she hasn't rested her chin on my shoulder, she almost has and this is a big gesture. And I can feel her belly pressing into my back. And I'm very happy with that. I'm very happy. And yes, I'm not going to, to lie, there's a part of me, yes, that thinks, yes alright, I did get to a point when I couldn't...stand to look at that belly, and all – I'm not proud of this – and all that it represented or whatever, but, I'm not going to pretend what has happened hasn't happened and maybe, yes, in three months, a year, I don't know, no-one knows the future, but right now I'm very happy to feel that belly in my back thank you, and I'm almost tempted to lean back into her, but I know how delicate this moment is and I know not to do that yet and I know that all of this is up to her and she's perhaps, I don't know, testing? I don't know, or something, so I don't lean back and her chin isn't on my shoulder but this is, you know I can feel something being said here so I just stand there cooking – watching my Salmon Teriyaki and after maybe thirty seconds of this she looks up at me and says 'You've always been a lucky cunt.'

And I have to laugh.

Because it's true.

I have.

I have always been a lucky cunt.

Pause.

FRANCIS: So I'm standing at this bus-stop and my feet are in concrete, they're made of lead, ice, and all around me the high street is flowing, buses coming and going and I can't move, don't get on them, people washing around me, flowing around me and I have no idea how long I'm there because things outside seem speeded up but things inside are moving slower than continents and I am terrified to the core of my body because I can feel the concrete creeping up my legs, I can feel the lead claiming me molecule by molecule, I can feel the ice slowly taking me over and I want to scream for help, cry I want to cry, I am shitting it in case it reaches my chest and I stop breathing, and I cannot move and I'm praying that it doesn't reach my lungs but I'm powerless to stop it and this small bloke bumps into this big bloke and knocks over his ice-cream. Just like that. Just bumps into him, no-one noticing, really, he just bumps into him and the ice-cream, it sort of topples, it topples into the gutter. And splats, comic really, this big bloke's ice-cream toppling off into the dirt. And this big bloke, who's with his girlfriend, and she seems very nice, this big bloke turns to the little bloke and, he's smiling the big bloke, but you can tell he's gutted, I mean you are aren't you, if something like that happens, you're gutted, and he's saying that the little bloke has to get him another. And the little bloke is saying no, because the big bloke wasn't watching where he was going, which is fair enough because I saw this, and the big bloke who's gutted is screaming at the little bloke, shoving him, and the little bloke is standing his ground but you can tell he's not up for this and the big bloke's girlfriend is shouting at the big bloke, telling him to stop, begging him, and I feel sorry for her because she's nice enough, and the big bloke now is shoving the little bloke, bouncing him off this plate-glass window. And now everyone has noticed. And the entire street has stopped. And the girlfriend and the big bloke

start a massive row. And the little bloke sees his chance
and he gets out of there. He just walks away. He hasn't
bargained for this, he's on his way to work, meet some
friends or something, a coffee, a drink I don't know, and
this big bloke notices he's gone and he's chasing after him
and suddenly I'm behind him, I'm behind this big bloke
because there is a panic in my guts and it's broad daylight,
but I've seen the look in the big bloke's eyes and it is pure
fire, pure fury and he reaches the little bloke who doesn't
know he's there and he runs up behind him and shoves
him with all his might – and again this is comic because
it's like he's in the playground – and this little bloke who
doesn't know he's there goes flying into this concrete post,
the side of his head straight on the edge and what is most
shocking is the noise. It's like this crack. Like you'd hit that
concrete with a hammer. And he's on the floor and there
is blood pouring, pumping out of this gash just above his
temple and he is grey, he is suddenly the colour of the
concrete. And we just stand there. Me and the big bloke
and his girlfriend. And I look up at him. At his face. And I
feel so sorry for him. His face. I wanted to almost hold his
hand, because he hadn't, this wasn't what he'd…

Second hangs in the air like breath.

And then they're off, him first, her still staring until the
pull, because he has her hand, until the pull yanks her
away and I just have time to see that she's terrified before
she's gone. Terrified of that grey face pumping blood,
terrified of that sound, that crack, and I'm on my knees and
I'm sitting him upright because somewhere in the back of
my mind I remember that if he bleeds into his brain he'll
go into a coma and I don't know how I know that but I do
and he's coming round and he's trying to get up and I get
him to stay where he is and I'm trying not to let him see
the shade of grey that he's become reflected in my face,
and I keep talking to him while the ambulance is on its
way and I've got no idea, no idea at all what I said, I can't
remember, but I do remember that after a while he's began

to realise that he does need an ambulance after all, coz at first he just wants to get up and go to work but now he's realised and he's sitting quietly and I'm talking away to him and I've got no idea what I said and he thanks me.

He's thanking me.

And I'm thinking what are you doing? Thanking me? Me? D'you know what I am? But he's still thanking me.

He's

thanking

me.

And I want to cry. I want to cry my eyes out like a little baby and hug this grey man through all the blood because he's sitting there with a cracked open head and he's thanking me, but I know that I don't deserve to even touch, to even think about touching this man's blood. And I'm in the ambulance with him. And I'm holding his hand. And he's got an oxygen mask on him and I explain to them that I shouldn't be there, that I'm nothing. I was just around, and they smile and say, 'keep hold of his hand,' and I do. And I think that my heart is breaking into two distinct pieces. I think that it is cracking. And I think that it is emptying of blood and that I might die in this ambulance because of an emptied heart. And I look at my feet. And there's no concrete. And they're not made of lead. They're not made of concrete. And I just hold his hand. I just hold his hand.

Pause.

LOUISE: So I'm watching this man cutting this other man's head off. And he's doing it with this knife that looks like a kitchen knife or something, which is completely inappropriate, so he's having to put a lot of work into it, he has to push hard down, and he's sawing but that's no good really, because the knife has no teeth, and he's pulling the head back and sawing with the knife and sort of twisting it every so often and it's taking ages and I'm eating Chicken Kiev with peas, potatoes and gravy and it tastes pretty bad because it's one of those ready meals, and I'm eating it off my lap because I'm in my bedroom at my computer watching this man cutting this man's head off and this is the fifth time I've watched it because I feel I'm very close to understanding something and the potatoes are stuck *justifies* together and I hate that and the TV is on and there's an interview, it's this documentary I recorded and they're interviewing these American soldiers and the chicken is, it's sort of re-constituted so it's a bit spongy which makes me feel a bit queasy. And I burn my tongue on the butter, which is really hot. And there are four men around this man, all dressed in black and wearing masks and you can tell that they're wondering if they should give him a hand because he's really having to hack to get through and there's white writing going along the bottom, a translation into English of a statement read over the top of this and I smell a bit. I do, I do smell, because I haven't had a wash in a few days, in fact, I haven't been out in a few days but I'm close to something, I can feel that I'm close to an understanding so I click on the rewind and start again and peas fall off my fork because I wasn't concentrating on what I was doing *justifiesthe* and I sort of wonder, absently, while it's rewinding because this is streaming and you have to wait, if this isn't wrong and if I'm not using all this as, as entertainment, which would be sick, but I don't think I am because I think I'm close to something *meanstheendsjustif* and I pick up the peas from the plate with my fork and put them into my mouth.

Beat.

MARK: And yes, alright, I admit it, I serve with a slight flourish, a flourish, alright, because I have decided to serve it with these beans, green beans, like those French beans I think they are and it looks, it looks, and these are fantastic, because the way I do them is I dip them in a sieve in boiling water and the moment they're back to the boil I pull them out – blanching, this is blanching, I'm blanching them – the moment they're back to the boil I whip them out and run them under the cold tap and then, and this is so fucking easy that it makes me guilty almost it's so easy, I sprinkle them with a little brown sugar, some roasted sesame seeds, which come in a bag, I mean they come in a fucking bag, I mean it's not as if I'm sitting here roasting them myself, and a little bit of Cajun spice – and the Japanese use something else which I don't know what the fuck it is so I always use Cajun spice which means with the spice and the sugar and the sesame seeds these beans are sweet and spicy and crunchy, so you have the pink of the salmon, the green of the beans, it looks fucking, the rice in a little dome and the Teriyaki drizzled, and so yes, there is a bit of a flourish when I lay these plates down and the look on her face – it's only slight – but she's impressed. And I know it's all worth it. And we sit down to eat. Chopsticks. We eat with chopsticks because why the fuck not?

LOUISE: And the beeping is the beeping of my answer machine and I know there are about ten messages on there and I know that they're all from work because I haven't been in for the last few days because, well I've been here. The peas aren't too bad actually and it starts again, the man having his head cut off and the man sort of stab-pushes into the man's neck, into the side of the man's neck and at that moment *fiesthemeansends* one of the men in black sort of lifts a foot, just sort of lifts a foot a little and then puts it back, and the man's hacking away and I can hear a new soldier on the telly and he's saying that he keeps a picture of the planes hitting the buildings on his locker to remind him why he's here, which seems a bit silly, the peas aren't too bad and I look around the room and there are headlines everywhere. Everywhere, papers. *Guardian. Daily Mail. Express. Sun, Mirror, Standard, Times, Telegraph, Financial Times. Independent.* Tons of headlines, all over my room, hundreds; six dead in Najaf, Brits held without access to lawyers, terror plot failed, House of Saud denies terror links, Mullahs must denounce terror, American troops rescue buffalo, refineries no longer a target and then…

then

I sort of see myself from the outside, d'you know what I mean? I sort of see me stinking and eating Chicken Kiev watching this man having his head cut off surrounded by headlines with the TV on white words streaming across the bottom of the monitor and it's as if I'm seeing it in slow motion, it's as if the sound has taken on a different quality in my ear, far away, / everything's far away *endsjustifiesthemeansendsjustifiesthemeansendsjust* and I turn my head

to

the

computer.

Because

FRANCIS: And I'm standing inside the curtain, I'm inside the curtain while he sits on the side of the bed and the nurse and doctor, they do things to him, he's so grey and I'm thinking any minute now they're going to tell me to get out, but they don't, they don't tell me to get out, they just tend this man and he's, honestly, he's smiling at them, he is, he's in this room smiling at them, not like I mean he's not mad, or it's not shock, he's just smiling his thank you to them and I'm thinking, 'Yes, yes, thank you,' and I want to pull the doctor away from him and thank her, I want to say, 'Thank you, thank you, this is what you do, this beautiful thing is what you do and I didn't even know this was happening, I didn't even know that this was here,' but I don't say anything because, look, because I don't even know this man and here I am on the inside of the curtain and they know I'm there, d'you see? they are moving around me knowing I'm there and getting on with their work / and they're not asking me to leave, d'you see? I'm on the inside of the curtain. And this man with the blood all over his clothes, he, he, he's looking at me and he's smiling that, he's smiling that… smile, and, and

MARK: Fucking, fucking, easy, easy fucking peasy, the flesh is breaking apart and I have to say it's cooked well, pink all the way through with perhaps a hint of a darker seam right through the centre, like wounded muscle, perfect and when you break this apart, I mean it's easy with chopsticks, when you break this apart it's like your eyes are eating, that's how, alright, that sounds stupid, but it's like you've tasted with your eyes and she's impressed. I know she's impressed. She's trying to be, all nonchalant, Miss Fucking-Nonchalant, but you know, I know, I can see and I'm not even, because this is such an easy dish and she's lifting, and this is it, she's lifting a piece of salmon with her chopsticks, and she's not very, I've always been deft with the old chopsticks but she's not, and, she's, it's almost to her mouth, it's, with her, the mouth, her lips pursing, reaching out as if she's going to kiss, almost, and, and, and it…drops. It drops with this splat onto her plate. And she's left there looking like she's going to kiss her chopsticks, and her face, her face is

a picture.

And suddenly I'm laughing. Because this is funny. This, you should see this, this is funny. And she looks at me, all sort of hurt, I mean not really, but like a child who's dropped her sandwich in a puddle, that second when they're almost deciding whether to cry or not and it just makes me laugh harder and there's a slight pause and then she starts laughing

LOUISE: and he sort of stab-pushes the knife into the side of the neck and the man sort of raises his foot and puts it down again and I rewind and the same thing happens and I rewind and the same thing happens *endsjustifiesthe means endsjustifiesthemeansendsjustifiesthemeansendsjustifiesthemeans* and I swing

my

head

to the

TV

because suddenly it's coming from outside of me, it's the soldier and he's just said it he's just said the ends justify the means. On telly. He's just said it and I realise, very slowly that I heard someone earlier say it, politician or, and maybe it's running through my mind because of that and I turn back *endsjustifiesthemeans* to *endsjustifiesthemeans* the *endsjustifiesthemeans* man *endsjustifiesthemeans* and I'm very close, I'm very, very close

MARK: and we're laughing

LOUISE: in the white writing

MARK: uncontrollably

LOUISE: I see in the white writing along the bottom of the screen

MARK: there are tears, there are tears running down

LOUISE: sort of stab-pushes the knife into the man's

neck and the man sort of

raises his foot, he

and in the white writing it's saying that force is justified by their ends the means

sort of

raises his foot

and I experience this moment

FRANCIS: and the nurse is telling me not to worry

LOUISE: of

FRANCIS: and that he's going to be fine, they just need to keep him in for observation and suddenly I'm

MARK: running down our cheeks

FRANCIS: crying

LOUISE: wondering how many of these stories

MARK: tears

LOUISE: these headlines I would find this phrase in, or variations of

FRANCIS: there are tears running down my cheeks

MARK: and it suddenly occurs to me that I'm not laughing at all

LOUISE: because I'm looking at this man and he's a bit, it was a surprise and it made him sort of step back, but he didn't want to step back but it was a surprise so, so he sort of, he lifts his foot

MARK: it suddenly occurs to me that I'm

FRANCIS: crying

MARK: crying

LOUISE: And it's such a human thing to do.

d'you know what I mean? To be surprised and then to try and cover it up, but not quite to be able to, this man, this man, this person and I experience a moment of

MARK: tears of pure ice, I'm crying ice

FRANCIS: and I feel

MARK: I feel, and this is just for a split second, I feel

FRANCIS: a moment of

MARK: absolute

LOUISE: shock

MARK: devastation

FRANCIS: hope

MARK: absolute devastation

LOUISE: washes over me

FRANCIS: flooding down my cheeks, these tears of hope, this is

MARK: absolute devastation, just for that split second, like a frame of a car accident inserted into a film, just that split second and it's as if I'm in death,

LOUISE: ends justify the means ends justifies the means ends justifies the means but

FRANCIS: this is

MARK: as if I'm living – just for that second – inside a scream, d'you know what I mean? inside, around me, inside me

LOUISE: this…boy

and my peas, my Chicken Kiev, my potatoes are spilling onto the floor because my muscles have gone slack, and part of me can feel the garlic butter scalding my leg but

FRANCIS: this is

LOUISE: this boy

because that's what he is, this boy raising his foot because he's…shocked, and I

can

not

move

FRANCIS: and this is

LOUISE: because I suddenly realise the complexity

MARK: a frame of absolute devastation that undercuts everything

LOUISE: the complexity of each individual

FRANCIS: hope

LOUISE: human and maybe they don't

MARK: and then it's back to the laughter

LOUISE: maybe they never do

FRANCIS: and I don't even know this man's name

LOUISE: maybe they never justify and it's the means that's important and the garlic butter is burning

MARK: back into the laughter and we're laughing and she's right

LOUISE: this boy

FRANCIS: this man

MARK: she is right

FRANCIS: this man's name, I don't even, but I

LOUISE: this silly boy.

FRANCIS: but I

MARK: I am a lucky cunt.

Pause.

MANDY: Afterwards I went for a walk. Didn't wanna go home. Him sitting there. Talking bollocks. I walked for miles. I wasn't scared. I just walked and walked and walked. And I could feel the night around me, brushing my skin, it was like it was brushing my skin. And all that's going through my mind, for some reason, is this thing my dad used to say when I was a kid. And for some reason I remember this, and this is from before he was a cunt, when he was a man, when he was a real, big man. He used to say that the reason the Soviet Bloc fell was because in nineteen eighty-nine there was a global nuclear war that killed every single man, woman and child on this planet. But it was such a massive shock that we didn't realise we was dead, so we just carried on with our lives. But our hearts knew there wasn't any point. That's why everything's so shit. Imagine saying that to a little girl. But I loved it. I thought it was so clever. And now, walking through this night, it's the only thing going through my head, again and again and again; we're all dead, we're all dead, we're all dead. And I'm in this park. And I don't even remember getting in, I mean I must've climbed over a wall or a gate, and they're big walls as well, but this park is huge. There's like whole hills in it, and woods, and all sorts, and I'm just wandering round this park, two, three o'clock in the morning, I don't know. And everything's old in here. And on top of this hill there's these old buildings and you know that in the day those buildings are open and that this is an important park and in the day those buildings are open to the public and it's tourists and stuff, but right now it's just me. Me and the park. And I sit down. But the place I sit in is no good because I've got a view of the buildings on the hill. So I move. I carry on walking till I find somewhere else, but that's no good coz I can see the gates. So I move and find somewhere else, but that's no good coz there's a view of Canary Wharf, so I move, but that's no good coz I can see some shops on the high street so I move but that's no good because I can see the wall of the park so I move but that's no good coz I can see a crane so I move but that's no good coz there's this office block and flats so I move and that's fine. That's fine. I can see no trace of civilisation whatsoever. And I just sit there. And I begin to think that I would like to live in this park. I begin to think of it, but I begin to think of it as a real possibility. And I'm thinking about how I could build a shelter here, and during the day I could hide out here and in the night I could wander round the park and I'm thinking I could catch squirrels or something, but I mean this, this, this is such a strong feeling, I mean this feels like a real possibility. And I feel alright. And the sun is coming up. And I realise that from where I'm sitting I can see people after all, now there's light, through the trees I can just, like, shops, the backs of these shops, and some parked cars and it's the city. It feels like the beginning of the city. But now I feel alright. I feel good now, I feel like maybe we're not dead after all. And this is, this is gonna sound silly, alright; but coz of how I'm feeling now, I pour my love into the city.

To help.

I try to help. Like it's a liquid. And I'm sitting there with the sun rising, pouring my love into the city.

That's what I'm doing.

And then I remember.

I remember.

Pause.

I always used to think there was grown-ups somewhere. D'you know what I mean, though? Someone in charge. Running the show, who knows what's best. I always thought there was grown-ups. Now I know there are no grown-ups. There's just us.

End

AFTER THE END

Characters

MARK

LOUISE

After the End was first produced at The Bush Theatre, in a Paines Plough / Bush Theatre co-production, on 28 July 2005, with the following cast:

MARK, Tom Brooke

LOUISE, Kerry Condon

Director Roxana Silbert

Designer Miriam Buether

Lighting Design Chahine Yavroyan

Sound Design Matt McKenzie

Beginning

MARK and LOUISE. A 1980s nuclear fallout shelter with a wheel-hatch in the ceiling, but in the present day. Bunks, table and chair, toilet area off and large metallic chest under the beds.

Pause.

MARK: I'm carrying you. I can't find my way because the streets, the houses, the houses were gone, the buildings were rubble, so I couldn't be sure and I'm panicking, I'm scared, there's bodies everywhere and just, the only sound is things burning and I can see the cloud rising and there was fires inside the, the cloud, inside it, beautiful, just unbelievable just, and I got to the junction and I thought 'Is this the fucking Junction?' there was no land marks, this is my fucking road and I've lived here for years but I didn't know if this was my fucking road even though I've lived here for years and I put you down next to this burnt lump, this body, charred, completely, like burnt wood, you know when it gets charred and it's cracked and you can break off a piece of charcoal, no skin, no clothes and her hands were almost ash, there was bits of her blowing away and I put you down next to this. And I'm clambering over the rubble trying to get higher to see if this is the fucking junction because if this isn't the fucking junction we're fucked, we're really fucked, the cloud is the only thing I can see above the fire and smoke and rubble and it's like it's rising with me and I'm thinking, okay, we've survived the blast, miracle, we've survived the fireball, miracle, but when that cloud starts to fall we're fucked, we're fucked, we're fucked unless we're in here. And then I see next door's…pattern on his drive, on his patio, it's a pattern, irregular sort of, it's a pattern but in the bit you walk on –

LOUISE: Crazy paving.

MARK: Yes, his crazy, yes, paving, his, yes, and I go back to you and I get there and the body is lifting itself up.

125

It's pushing itself up. It's trying to push itself, but it's crumbling. It's pushing itself up and its fingers are crumbling and it's pushing itself up on its palms but its palms are crumbling, but it's still pushing itself and a bit by the elbow breaks off and I can see meat and bone and I run. I run off. I ran off and left you there.

LOUISE: But you came back.

MARK: Yes. I saw the crazy paving and I came back. And I picked you up. And I brought you here.

Beat.

LOUISE: Thank you.

MARK: You're welcome.

Silence.

LOUISE: But I'm starting my new job on Monday.

MARK: Yeah, well that's –

I think that's probably…

Yeah, no.

*   *   *

MARK is pulling cans and supplies out of the metal chest, talking to LOUISE over his shoulder. She sits staring at him, lost in thought.

MARK: Chilli…

Chilli…

Chilli…

Baked beans, baked beans with sausages…

Chilli…

Tuna…

More tuna, with mayonnaise, I don't think that's very –

Chilli…

She gets up and comes over to him.

LOUISE: I've got your number.

Beat.

MARK: What?

LOUISE: I wasn't leaving without, I mean I've got your number, Mark.

MARK: Oh, I know.

LOUISE: I've got your

MARK: Oh, I know, I know

LOUISE: coz I feel I didn't really, last night I didn't really

MARK: Leaving does are always

LOUISE: I didn't really, they are, yeah, leaving does are always, did I talk to you? because

MARK: we talked

LOUISE: We did, yeah, that's right, but, because I don't think I got the chance to talk to you properly last night

MARK: Oh, no, no, you had lots, I mean you had lots, loads of people, you can't

LOUISE: I wasn't just gonna, but I'm saying I had your number, so it's not as if

MARK: Oh God no.

LOUISE: I mean I wasn't, I don't really remember

MARK: no, no, I know, well, you were a bit

LOUISE: I was but, I wasn't just never ever again or something, I mean

MARK: No, we're friends, Jesus, no, I know

LOUISE: Just so you know.

MARK: Oh I do know, definitely.

LOUISE: Do you?

MARK: Definitely. We're friends, I mean, we're friends it's not just

LOUISE: Exactly. Definitely.

Beat.

Did we row a little?

MARK: No.

LOUISE: Did we?

MARK: No, no, well…

LOUISE: We did, didn't we. God, not again.

MARK: Well, yes, we did a little.

LOUISE: (*Laughing a little.*) Jesus, sorry

MARK: (*Laughing with her.*) no, no, it was just

LOUISE: We're like kids or something, God, I'm sorry, was I an arsehole?

MARK: no, honestly it was about nothing

LOUISE: my memory is like in and out, was it about nothing? what was it about?

MARK: Nothing.

LOUISE: Really?

MARK: it was about nothing, I mean so small, nothing at all

LOUISE: Jesus, just arguing over nothing

MARK: honestly don't worry

LOUISE: like kids or something,

MARK: and you'd had a few

LOUISE: someone should smack us across the back of the legs

MARK: so I know you didn't mean anything

LOUISE: I really didn't, God I'm sorry

MARK: because, no, don't apologise because I'm saying, I know you didn't mean

LOUISE: I didn't.

MARK: to be rude

LOUISE: I wasn't rude.

MARK: You called me a cunt.

Beat.

LOUISE: That was rude.

MARK: It was a little.

LOUISE: Sorry.

MARK: It was a little

LOUISE: Yeah, I know, I'm sorry, I really am, fucking hell, I really am

MARK: Oh look, I don't think you meant it to be so

LOUISE: when I have a few

MARK: cruel

LOUISE: Cruel?

MARK: or harsh, I mean

LOUISE: it was more like you're a cunt or something, like you just call someone a cunt and you don't really mean

MARK: You remember?

LOUISE: Pieces, I remember

MARK: that's why I left the pub after you, to say

LOUISE: I don't remember leaving, Jesus,

MARK: I wanted to say sorry, or, and that's when

LOUISE: it happened?

MARK: when it happened, yes, so we were lucky, when you think about it, we were lucky we rowed

LOUISE: Rowing as a good thing?

MARK: rowing as a good thing, yeah, exactly, because I think we were sheltered by, wall, a wall or something so –

Look, let's leave it, we need to get on. Imperative, so

LOUISE: Exactly.

Jesus Christ, yeah, exactly.

Pause.

But I'm just saying that I wasn't fucking off and not saying goodbye, because I have your number so I wasn't actually saying goodbye.

MARK: I never feel like I'm saying goodbye to someone I really like.

LOUISE: Exactly. That's exactly, that's how I feel.

MARK: I'm really glad we talked about this.

He goes back to sorting.

LOUISE: D'you want a hand?

MARK: What?

LOUISE: Sorting or…

MARK: No it's fine I've…

LOUISE: I could help

MARK: got it all

LOUISE: I could help or something.

> *Beat.*

MARK: Yeah. Yeah, okay. I'm, well I'm just sorting it into

LOUISE: Rations?

MARK: rations, yeah, it's rations, yeah, that's right, it's rations really.

LOUISE: So it's days of the week?

MARK: Yeah, and different foodstuffs, varied, variations. We're a bit short on food. We'll be fine. I mean there's enough for one comfortably and we can stretch, we can make it –

LOUISE: My brother's dead.

D'you think my brother's –

Probably.

Don't feel

anything.

> *Pause.*

MARK: D'you think you're suppressing…

LOUISE: No. I just don't feel anything.

MARK: I cried.

LOUISE: Did you?

MARK: Sorry. I don't know why I said that, sorry, shit. Before you came round. Maybe relief at getting in out of, or something.

LOUISE: maybe I'm concussed

MARK: I don't think that affects your feelings.

LOUISE: What was it?

She sits down and starts sorting with him.

Do you know?

MARK: Terrorists. Probably.

It was small. It looked smaller than, I dunno, but I mean it must've, so…

Suitcase nuke.

LOUISE: In a suitcase?

MARK: No, no, they just,

LOUISE: How do you know it was in…?

MARK: No, it wasn't, no, that's what they call them. You know, they're like a portable device that you set off yourself. That's why they say suitcase because like maybe you could carry one in

LOUISE: Right. Why is there nothing on the radio?

MARK: Could be anything.

LOUISE: Like what?

MARK: EMP.

LOUISE: What's that?

MARK: Electro magnetic pulse. Maybe. Knocks out all electrics in a certain area, maybe the masts, the transmitters

LOUISE: Is that likely?

MARK: No.

Beat.

We'll keep trying.

LOUISE: Every three hours. That's what you said.

MARK: Yeah. Every three

LOUISE: I'm glad you know about this stuff, Mark.

MARK: Ah, yeah. Well, you know. My shelter. So…

LOUISE: So is this the menu for the next two weeks?

MARK: Yes. Two weeks.

Sorry. There's a lot of chilli.

LOUISE: I like Chilli. We can heat the shelter at the same time.

MARK: Yeah.

Beat.

How?

LOUISE: With all the farting.

Beat.

It's a joke.

MARK: Oh yeah.

He laughs. She smiles. They carry on sorting. Suddenly he makes a farting noise. It is not funny, but she laughs anyway.

LOUISE: You were right.

I mean all this. Shelter and –

MARK: Louise –

LOUISE: You were though, weren't you. We all took the piss. We laughed when you bought a flat with a shelter in the garden

MARK: Christ, that doesn't matter now, and that isn't, actually – I keep saying this – that isn't why I bought the flat

LOUISE: I know

MARK: I bought the flat because I like it and it's not too bad for transport and it happened to have an old shelter in the back

LOUISE: Yeah, but you kept it.

MARK: I kept it, yes, rather than tear out

LOUISE: You kept it stocked up. In preparation –

MARK: Which I kept stocked up because the world has gone fucking insane!

They sort.

Look, it wasn't about the shelter. It was because I got the shelter. I mean if it'd been someone else everyone'd be all 'Oh, isn't that great, isn't that funny' and all that old whatever, but because I get it

LOUISE: Oh, come on.

MARK: What?

LOUISE: Oh, come on Mark, that's not true.

MARK: It is. I mean I'm not being, it is, because if Francis had got it everyone'd think it was hilarious and really clever but because it's me

LOUISE: Mark, it just seemed a bit

MARK: What?

LOUISE: a bit, well, paranoid.

MARK: Paranoid? They've let off a nuclear bomb!

LOUISE: I know, okay, I'm saying it seemed, at the time it seemed

MARK: Well it seemed wrong, then, didn't it.

LOUISE: That's what I'm saying, I'm saying you were right.

MARK: Right but paranoid.

LOUISE: Because, alright, but some of the things you say sometimes

MARK: are right, were right, have turned out right.

LOUISE: Well, maybe they are

MARK: Well, who do you think did this then?

LOUISE: I know, I'm saying

MARK: Well I tell you what, whoever it was, you can bet your life they had beards.

LOUISE: Oh, Mark.

MARK: Alright, sorry, no I mean, fair enough

LOUISE: For Christ's sake

MARK: Well, actually, now that we're at it, who do you think did this?

LOUISE: I know, Mark, that's what I'm saying, I'm confused, I don't fucking know, but what I'm saying is

MARK: What?

Beat.

LOUISE: Look, there's all these people, right, who are just fucking saying I know what's best and you do what I say or I'll shoot you in the fucking head, on both sides, Mark, on both fucking sides, and I just don't think that the best way to combat them is to start saying you do what I say or I'll shoot you in the fucking head.

MARK: How do you fight, then?

LOUISE: I don't –

MARK: No, I'm interested.

LOUISE: I don't know, Mark, I'm saying I'm confused, I'm saying this is what I believe and meanwhile my friends are either dead or screaming in agony or

MARK: Because that's called burying your head in the sand. I'm sorry, but it is.

LOUISE: Oh, for fuck's sake.

MARK: Which is what I refused to do and which is what I was laughed at for.

LOUISE: You weren't laughed at

MARK: and you can sit there and criticise governments and politicians and whatever, and that's easy, to do from pubs and trendy bars and sitting rooms, but at the end of the day you have to do something, the reality is tough, you have to close borders, imprison if you have to

LOUISE: Jesus, Mark, you're sounding just a little bit fascist.

MARK: And that is exactly, that is exactly the kind of comment and attitude

LOUISE: I don't mean –

MARK: It's a war! It's a war and just because there hadn't been an attack like this didn't mean there wasn't going to be, and what do you want to do with that time, just sit and accept

LOUISE: I know

MARK: just wait there drinking, laughing, smoking, taking the piss

LOUISE: I know, Mark, I'm saying

MARK: Look at where we are!

LOUISE: I'm saying I fucking know, for fuck's sake, I'm saying I fucking –

MARK: Well don't start swearing at me all over again!

They sort in silence.

LOUISE: I'm saying I know.

They sort.

Did you hurt your back?

MARK: What?

LOUISE: Did you hurt your back, Mark?

MARK: Well, I think

LOUISE: What?

MARK: I think I grazed it.

LOUISE: Why didn't you tell me?

MARK: I don't know, I –

LOUISE: Let me see it. Let me see it!

He turns round and lifts his shirt at the back.

Jesus.

MARK: It's nothing it's –

She touches it.

Ow!

LOUISE: Looks like a burn.

She goes to the chest, pulls out some ointment and bandages. She is at his back, starts treating him.

Is it radiation or...?

MARK: Don't remember, I mean it was all, maybe it's a graze

LOUISE: It's a burn.

MARK: getting you in, it's a tight, maybe I grazed –

LOUISE: It's a fucking burn, Mark.

Looks sore.

MARK: It's a little –

Ow.

Yes, it's a little.

LOUISE: You should've told me. You fucking tell me about things like this.

MARK: Okay.

LOUISE: You fucking tell me. I mean it, Mark, you fucking –

MARK: Okay!

Pause.

LOUISE: Okay?

MARK: Okay.

She has finished. He turns around.

You know, I think we're going to be alright.

* * *

They lie on their bunks, wrapped up, cold.

MARK: Cold.

LOUISE: Yeah.

Beat.

MARK: We have to save the gas. I'm not being bossy, Louise.

LOUISE: Oh, I know.

MARK: and the fumes are not so, so it's best

LOUISE: We're fine like this.

MARK: Yeah.

Yeah, fine like this.

Pause.

And sorry about the water as well

LOUISE: Oh, no don't

MARK: I mean I wasn't being

LOUISE: Oh, I know, Mark

MARK: bossy or, we just have to save

LOUISE: I know you weren't, and I didn't mean

MARK: because we can't really use it for

LOUISE: I didn't mean to snap

MARK: washing, you didn't snap.

LOUISE: I did and I'm sorry.

MARK: No, course you didn't.

LOUISE: I mean drinking's more important.

MARK: It is.

Maybe we could wash a little, though. Special occasions. You didn't snap.

Silence.

Are you thinking about Francis?

LOUISE: What?

MARK: No, I mean, you know. Are you?

LOUISE: Am I thinking about Francis?

MARK: Because I just noticed in the pub –

LOUISE: What?

MARK: No, I mean I just noticed that you were friendly.

LOUISE: Well, we're friends

MARK: with him, oh no, I know, I mean…no, no, I'm just saying in case you wanted

LOUISE: What?

MARK: To talk. I thought you might want to talk about it. Or something.

LOUISE: D'you think he's dead?

No answer.

I'm really glad you brought this flat, you know.

MARK: Well. You know what we say in the reprographics department; tedious but lucrative.

Pause.

Are you thinking about Francis? Coz I mean if you wanted to talk –

LOUISE: I'm thinking about my brother.

MARK: Right.

D'you want to talk, or…

LOUISE: No. Thank you.

Silence. He has an idea.

MARK: They send the first two astronauts to Mars, right, and they're in their little – it's a man and a woman – they're in their little unit and it's a six-month flight to get there and they've been crammed into this capsule for six months together, a man and a woman, and they're there in their little unit and it's the first night and the heating's broken down and they're in their bunks freezing away, she's on the top bunk and he's on the bottom bunk and they're both really cold and it's really quiet and they're both not saying anything and after a while she says, 'I'm cold' and he says 'Yeah, me too' and there's a silence and she leans over the bunk and says to him 'Would you get me another blanket?' and he looks up at her and he says 'You know, just for tonight, why don't we pretend like we're man and wife?' And she looks at him and she thinks and she says 'Yeah. Okay. Just for tonight' and he says 'Good. Now get your own damn blanket.'

Pause. He laughs a little to indicate it was a joke. Nothing.

It was a joke, it was…

Pause.

Shit. Sorry.

Fuck, sorry.

I'm sorry, Louise, it's, I wasn't, it's, I wasn't, I wasn't –

LOUISE: Fucking hell, Mark.

MARK: Oh my God I am so

LOUISE: Jesus, where did you get that one?

MARK: Louise, I am so, so…sorry, I am

LOUISE: That's fucking terrible.

She starts laughing.

MARK: I don't know why I said

Laughing harder.

Louise?

LOUISE: That's the most stupid fucking, inappropriate

She can't stop laughing.

MARK: Louise?

LOUISE: You're so mental.

Doesn't know how to take this. Decides it's positive. Starts laughing as well.

MARK: Yeah.

Yeah I know.

They are both laughing.

Fucking mental.

The laughter subsides. Silence.

I touched your breast.

LOUISE: (*Beat.*) What?

MARK: By accident. I didn't mean to it was, I was carrying you and your arm was hanging down and I realised where I was holding you and it was your breast.

I just wanted to say I'm sorry, and for it to be, well, open or

LOUISE: Right.

MARK: It wasn't anything like that, I just couldn't move my arm, because the cloud and, oh fuck, why am I saying this?

LOUISE: Why are you saying this?

MARK: I just wanted –

LOUISE: It's okay.

MARK: shit, I just wanted

LOUISE: Go to sleep, Mark.

MARK: That's a good idea, sleep, yes. Good.

Silence.

LOUISE: What do you think's out there? Now? I mean people and that. I mean d'you think there's people dying up there and –

There is, isn't there.

MARK: Best not to think.

LOUISE: No. No, sorry.

MARK: Enough on our plates.

LOUISE: Yeah. What's it going to be like after? I mean d'you think we'll all be like, will it be the end of things, will it be really military or, I mean will it be like checkpoints and things?

MARK: Dunno.

LOUISE: Will we just have to imprison people if we're suspicious of them or something, I mean will we all be bastards?

MARK: I think we'll take…precautions.

LOUISE: D'you think there's people searching?

MARK: Not yet. Not for a long time yet.

LOUISE: So people are just going to be lying up there? Dying. Screaming.

Beat.

MARK: Best not think about out there. Got to concentrate on getting through. Hard enough in here, eh. We'll be fine, but…best not think about that, out there.

Silence. Another idea.

There are these three vets, right and one's – veterinary surgeons – and one's an – not like veterans, army or, but you probably know that – so one's an alcoholic, one's a drug addict and the other is addicted to pornography and when they get paid the first vet says to the second vet 'Right, I've got this idea' he –

Beat. He looks over. She is crying. He immediately gets off his bunk and sits on the edge of hers. Puts his arm around her. She leans into him.

There, there.

There, there.

Middle

LOUISE: I hate it.

MARK: Well you haven't –

LOUISE: I fucking hate it.

MARK: That's a bit

LOUISE: I fucking

MARK: negative.

LOUISE: hate it.

MARK: Why don't you just –

LOUISE: because I fucking –

MARK: You didn't let me finish my sentence, Louise!

Beat.

LOUISE: Finish your sentence, then.

MARK: Why don't you just try it?

LOUISE: Because I fucking hate it.

Pause.

MARK: We have to do something.

LOUISE: Not that.

MARK: We have to keep occupied, do things.

LOUISE: Not Dungeons and fucking Dragons. Do you play that?

MARK: No, when I was a kid –

LOUISE: Do you dress up like a pixie or something?

MARK: No, no, for God's sake, Louise and I mean you don't dress up you just, look, I'm just, it's just a suggestion because we –

LOUISE: Why haven't you got any other games?

MARK: It was built in the eighties. It's an eighties game.

LOUISE: You brought it two years ago, why aren't there games from other eras, why aren't there some nineties games?

MARK: It seemed sort of – what nineties games?

LOUISE: Pictionary.

MARK: fitting, it sort of fitted with, you know, the, the

LOUISE: Apocalyptic

MARK: nuclear, because, no not, because when I was a kid

LOUISE: You're not a kid.

MARK: I know, but when –

LOUISE: So you shouldn't be playing Dungeons and fucking Dragons.

Beat.

When can we try the radio?

MARK: We tried it two hours ago.

LOUISE: What I said was when can we –

MARK: What's three minus two?

LOUISE: One.

MARK: You can try the radio in one hour then.

LOUISE: I don't have a watch.

MARK: I do, I can tell you.

LOUISE: It's like time's turned off. Doesn't it bother you that there's nothing on the radio?

MARK: I've made you a character, she's an elf called –

LOUISE: I don't want to be a fucking elf!

MARK: You could be a dwarf.

I think you're being negative.

Beat.

Yes. Yes, actually, it bothers me. But what am I going to do about it?

Beat.

LOUISE: Sorry.

MARK: It's only been three days

LOUISE: Feels like three years.

MARK: We have to look after each other.

LOUISE: I know.

I know. I'm sorry, Mark.

Pause.

MARK: When I was a kid I used to love it. Alright, yes, I'm admitting –

Escape or something, I don't…

I associate it with caravans. I've never been in a caravan. I think it was because a mate of mine used to go on holiday in a caravan and we never went on holiday and I always thought what it'd be like to be in a caravan. He'd always tell me stories of getting a girlfriend in this caravan –

LOUISE: This isn't a caravan.

And I'm not your girlfriend.

Silence.

MARK: Would you do it if Francis asked you?

LOUISE: Oh, for God's sake

MARK: No, I'm just wondering

LOUISE: No you're not

MARK: I am

LOUISE: You're not because you're mental and that's a loaded question designed to feed into your paranoia about Francis.

MARK: I don't have paranoia about Francis and this is, actually this is just like Jess' party.

Beat.

LOUISE: Jess' party?

MARK: Yes.

LOUISE: Jess' party?

MARK: Yes.

LOUISE: Why are you bringing up Jess' party?

MARK: Because –

LOUISE: What the fuck has Jess' party got to do with anything?

MARK: Because at Jess' party, at Jess' party you were taking the piss

LOUISE: that was months ago, I mean do you ever let go of anything?

MARK: taking the piss and belittling, you were –

LOUISE: I was belittling?

MARK: Yes, you were belittling me.

LOUISE: At Jess' party, I was belittling you?

MARK: Yes.

LOUISE: What about you!

MARK: What about me?

LOUISE: You were acting like a freak.

MARK: Me?

LOUISE: Like we're all having a drink and a laugh and suddenly everything I say you're like jumping on, no you don't really think that Louise, that's not you Louise, why are you talking about Footballer's Wives, Louise.

MARK: You were being fake.

LOUISE: Fake?

MARK: You were pissed though, so I

LOUISE: Fake? Who the fuck are you to decide if I'm fake or not?

MARK: You weren't being you.

LOUISE: You don't decide who I am, I decide

MARK: We'd talked, when you first started, we'd talked about so many

LOUISE: And I enjoyed those, I mean I really, we had some good

MARK: Stuff that matters, like

LOUISE: And I do, I like that, but who the fuck are you to decide who I am

MARK: cloning and global, and now you're talking about this irrelevant

LOUISE: I was just being normal, getting on with people –

MARK: Upgrading.

LOUISE: (*Beat.*) What?

MARK: You were upgrading.

LOUISE: Oh, for fuck's sake.

MARK: No, its fine, that's what happens, people want more, better friends and

LOUISE: For fuck's sake!

MARK: And you started it all with that stupid first impressions game.

Beat.

LOUISE: Oh my God.

MARK: What?

LOUISE: Mark, is that what that was all about?

MARK: Well, don't say it like it's petty.

LOUISE: It is petty.

MARK: You laughed

LOUISE: Fucking hell.

MARK: You laughed, Louise.

LOUISE: Mark, you are mad.

MARK: What's your first impression of Sarah, Louise – bit cheeky: what's your first impression of Gary, Louise – a good laugh

LOUISE: I like you, Mark, but you are totally insane.

MARK: what's your first impression of Francis, Louise – bit of a bastard, watch out for that one

LOUISE: I'm in bunker with an insane man.

MARK: what's your first impression of Mark, Louise, and you just laughed.

LOUISE: What's wrong with that?

MARK: You laughed!

LOUISE: It was a warm laugh.

MARK: And everyone else laughed with you.

LOUISE: I called Francis a bastard.

MARK: A bastard is good, I would've liked bastard

LOUISE: You're not a bastard

MARK: but with me you just laughed

LOUISE: Because I liked you and it was a warm

MARK: and everyone else laughed as if we all knew what a prick –

LOUISE: I mean is that what that all that was about?

MARK: So tell me now then?

Beat.

Go on.

Tell me now. Tell me now what you thought when you first met me.

Pause. She comes close to him.

LOUISE: Mark, I want you to know that I know exactly what I'm saying when I say this. I'm not telling you because I don't want to and because I don't have to, and I'm not playing Dungeons and Dragons because I don't want to and I don't have to. I really like you. I really think you're a good person and we had some good conversations, really good, but I think you are fucking mental and you're a control freak.

She goes and lies on her bunk. Silence.

MARK: We have to play Dungeons and Dragons. It's important.

Louise?

It's very important.

Are you playing?

LOUISE: No.

Pause.

MARK: Well

I'm going

to have to insist.

LOUISE: (*Beat.*) What?

MARK: I'm,

you know, I'm going to have to insist.

LOUISE: You're going to have to insist?

MARK: Yes. Sorry.

LOUISE: You're going to have to insist that I play Dungeons and Dragons?

MARK: We have to, it's important that we keep occupied, this is actually a really important –

LOUISE: How? How are you going to insist?

MARK: I'm trying –

LOUISE: No, I'm interested. How, Mark?

Beat.

MARK: This is my shelter.

I mean I've not said that before, coz I don't want you to feel…

LOUISE: Are you going to kick me out?

MARK: to feel, no, of course I'm not –

LOUISE: Are you going to hit me?

MARK: No, no of course I wouldn't, never, no –

LOUISE: Are you going to starve me?

No answer.

Are you going to starve me?

No answer.

Mark, are you going to starve me?

MARK: It's my food. Isn't it.

I want to do what's best for you. You know. Like when I carried you –

LOUISE: Like when you touched my breast?

No answer.

This dream of yours. In the caravan. What happened after you played the game? What did the girlfriend do then?

We could play I Spy.

MARK: Okay, then.

LOUISE: I spy with my little eye something beginning with 'N'.

MARK: Nuclear fallout shelter.

LOUISE: Yes.

MARK: Look, Louise. I am –

I am going to have to insist.

LOUISE: Go on then.

Fucking go on then.

You're gonna be really fucking sorry.

MARK: What does that mean?

No answer.

Louise? What does that –?

I'm not bothered, I mean –

Louise?

*   *   *

Morning. LOUISE is brushing her teeth.

MARK: I wasn't.

LOUISE: You were.

MARK: I wasn't!

LOUISE: I don't care.

MARK: But I wasn't –

LOUISE: I don't care, Mark.

MARK: But I wasn't.

LOUISE: Then why was the bed shaking?

Beat.

MARK: I was scratching.

LOUISE: Really?

MARK: Look I was, I was –

LOUISE: Scratching the bishop?

MARK: I was scratching!

LOUISE: Look, I don't care.

MARK: I do, I do care a lot. I would never do anything –

LOUISE: Except deny me food.

MARK: Is

is that why you're saying –

LOUISE: No.

MARK: because

LOUISE: I said no.

MARK: I mean it, Louise, because, that's, this is a serious, and I'm not denying –

LOUISE: You are.

MARK: I'm denying you some food, but I'm not denying you all food.

LOUISE: A couple of mouthfuls of rice for a whole day?

MARK: Well that's up to you, look that's beside, I wasn't, I wasn't

LOUISE: Look, just forget it, Mark, everyone likes the odd wank now and –

MARK: I wasn't! Is this something to do with

LOUISE: Just do it in the toilet.

MARK: Is it, Louise? The food or

LOUISE: Didn't I just say no?

Pause.

MARK: I wasn't.

LOUISE: Well, forget it, then

MARK: Yeah, but

LOUISE: because if you weren't it's not a problem.

MARK: Not 'if' I wasn't, I wasn't –

LOUISE: Well good, then.

MARK: No, because –

LOUISE: Isn't it good?

MARK: Yes, good, but –

LOUISE: Good, then.

MARK: Yeah, but –

LOUISE: Alright, then.

Pause.

MARK: Do you believe me?

LOUISE: Yes, Mark, I believe you, you were scratching.

MARK: You don't believe me.

LOUISE: I don't give a shit, actually

MARK: So you don't believe me.

LOUISE: I'm agreeing, I'm agreeing with what you want me to say.

MARK: Yeah, but you still think –

LOUISE: No, I was mistaken, I was wrong.

MARK: You don't think that. You don't believe me.

Beat.

This is how, this is where, this is where I am

LOUISE: Just leave it, will you?

MARK: Coz you're fucking so...you're so fucking...

So...

You're not quite as...

as you think, you know.

LOUISE: Mark? I'm sorry.

Silence.

MARK: You're not sorry.

You're not sorry, not for me. Not for me. What you think of me. The way you think of me...

He is crying.

Just some fucking...

LOUISE: Mark?

Mark?

MARK: I'm nothing, am I. Just a fucking little fucking...

He cannot speak.

LOUISE: Mark? Oh, Jesus, look I'm sorry.

Mark? I am, I'm really sorry, I was just –

You're not giving me any food, you fucking –

Look, I'm sorry. I was just winding you up, I –

MARK sorts himself out.

Mark, we're friends, we are, Mark, I'm just, it's just here. Being in here I feel…mental. I feel like my mind is being squashed. And I do

trust you.

Okay?

Okay, Mark?

Pause. He is looking at her.

Okay?

MARK: You made me sick in the pub.

LOUISE: (*Beat.*) What?

MARK: You, in the pub, you looked so fucking stupid.

LOUISE: Mark –

MARK: Grinning at him like a

LOUISE: What are you –

MARK: like a fucking cat, all dopey-eyed, you looked stupid

LOUISE: Mark?

MARK: Just fucking standing there gazing at him, gazing, just, you just, in front of everyone, everyone

LOUISE: Mark?

MARK: Francis, fucking Francis, like he's so clever, like, oh
you're so fucking clever, Francis, you're so –

Beat.

Sometimes I used to look at Francis. Sometimes I used to
look at him smiling there and I'd think to myself 'The only
reason you've got any of this is because I don't come up
behind you with an ice-pick and shove it into the base of
your skull. The only reason you're so wonderful is because
I don't follow you home one evening and turn you into a
paraplegic by stabbing you in the spine.'

Well he's dead. So who's clever now?

*   *   *

*MARK cooking rice on a Calor gas burner. LOUISE entirely aware
of the food, even when she is trying not to be.*

MARK: ...if you have a society, right, who is good, who is a
good, a good

LOUISE: Define good?

MARK: I'm about to define, Louise, if you'd let me, I'm
about to define. If you have, well democracy for starters,
you know, who feel that people, people can be free and,
women for a start, who treat women like people, there's,
and where you have rights and whatever, a legal system
without corruption or where you can be equal

LOUISE: Where's that then?

MARK: and then you have these other – alright, fair
enough, but I'm not saying perfection – you have these
other societies that aren't like, that are repressive and
dictatorships and where people are tortured

LOUISE: Or starved.

MARK: Alright, starved, they are, and then this first society, the good one, fair enough not perfect because that doesn't make sense, they have all the power, this first society has all the power but because of the way things are, all of our

LOUISE: Decadence?

MARK: Alright, I shouldn't've used that word, but yes, fuck it, decadence.

LOUISE: Decadence.

MARK: Yeah alright, I'm saying that fair enough

LOUISE: The queers and the blacks.

MARK: No, don't because I'm not

LOUISE: Go on.

MARK: No, because I'm not, that's not

LOUISE: Go on.

MARK: Yeah, but no, because –

alright we are a certain way, the people who live in that society

LOUISE: The good society.

MARK: Yeah, the good society, that society can't use its power to

LOUISE: Force.

MARK: Coerce, Louise, the societies, coerce and help

LOUISE: Help?

MARK: them to be

LOUISE: Help?

MARK: better than they have been and give people, the people within it rights.

But now…

Now that things have changed, we can see how stupid
we've been

LOUISE: by not dominating other countries.

MARK: Well yeah, but you don't have to put it like –

If you have power then you should use it. You have a
responsibility to use it. For good.

Beat.

LOUISE: Shall I tell you what I think?

*He begins to dole out the rice onto two plates, a healthy portion
for him, four dessertspoonfuls for her.*

MARK: Go on.

She stares.

Go on.

LOUISE: I think…

I think, it's easy to say things. Alright, I'm admitting that.
It's easy to have an opinion when no-one's testing,

MARK: Exactly.

LOUISE: before, and now that people are dead, I mean I don't
know what I feel, I mean my brother, I keep thinking
about did he get home and is he okay and I know my
friends, some of my friends are, and if I let it that can make
me, I can get really fucking angry

MARK: thank you, which is what I'm saying

LOUISE: but that doesn't, hang on, Mark, hold on, I'm saying
that doesn't affect what's right and wrong and maybe this is
when it matters anyway or something, I mean just because
some nutcase lets off a fucking bomb doesn't mean you
should go around being a bastard and fucking with the
brain of the entire world and saying right you do this or
I'll kill you and your family and everyone you know. You

either believe in something or you don't. Not just when you feel like it. When it's convenient.

He takes out an apple. Cuts a tiny slice off and puts it on the side of her plate. Puts the rest with his stuff.

I think,

He doles out the chilli, the entire contents on his plate, one spoon on her rice.

The only way people can destroy you is if you let them make you become something else.

He has finished doling out the food and now holds the plates.

MARK: That's easy for you to say isn't it. 'Don't become something else.' 'Be yourself.' You've got everything. People like you, have…

People want to be with you. When you walk into the pub people think 'Oh great, Louise is here.' Your laugh, your smile. You know how to dress, you know what to say to people, what to think, what to believe. You've friends, good friends real friends and you enjoy being with them and they love being with you, you don't sit there thinking 'What the fuck and I going to say, these are my only friends I've got and I don't even know what to say to them, I'm making my own friends feel uncomfortable.' You laugh. You smile. And people look at your smile and they think that it's the best thing that they've ever seen. They think that it makes them look like chunks of coal, but they want to be near, even if it hurts them, even if it kills them and turns their souls into pieces of dust.

Puts food back into the box. Chains and padlocks it. Hold the plate out to her.

Anyway. Everything's fucked. Out there. Isn't it.

He hands her the plate. She takes it and they sit down to eat in silence. She wolfs down every morsel, but when it is finished it is only enough food to remind her of how hungry she is. She stares at him eating his food, methodically. She stares. Suddenly she lunges for his food. He manages to get the plate on the floor and keep her from it. He pushes her away. They stand staring at each other. She goes for the food again, but again he pushes her away. Pause.

LOUISE: Please.

MARK: I'm just trying to do what's best.

*   *   *

They are playing Dungeons and Dragons. He reads.

MARK: 'You come out of the forest and suddenly the Keep is in front of you, like a ragged and ancient tooth on the hillside, jutting up into the night sky. It's covered in vines and ivy and bits of it are crumbling and the ancient path wends up to the portcullis. On either side of the portcullis are two forbidding statues of warriors, suggesting the ancient civilisation that once inhabited the keep, long since past. An eerie glow exudes from these statues bathing the entrance in a dull light and there are glints of moonlight –'

LOUISE: What do you mean 'like a tooth?

MARK: That's what it looks like.

LOUISE: It looks like a tooth?

MARK: Yes.

LOUISE: Like a tooth?

MARK: It's not white, it's just the shape is

LOUISE: Pointed?

MARK: No, not, not a pointed, not a fang, I didn't say fang

LOUISE: It's not just fangs that

MARK: Like a front tooth, a bottom front tooth.

LOUISE: Right. I still don't get it.

MARK: Get what?

LOUISE: Why have they shaped it like a tooth?

MARK: They haven't shaped it like a tooth, it's just a way of describing it.

LOUISE: You said –

MARK: That's just describing, it's an old tower, it's just this old tower

LOUISE: Alright, I get it.

MARK: it's an ancient tower that's sticking up

LOUISE: I get it, alright.

MARK: It's the ancient tower of an ancient civilisation long since deserted –

LOUISE: Is it deserted?

MARK: Well, that's what you have to find out.

LOUISE: Can I find out by asking you?

MARK: No, you have to go in –

LOUISE: Alright, I go in.

MARK: You can't just go in.

LOUISE: You just

MARK: Not just like that, Louise, you can't just

LOUISE: Fucking hell, you just

MARK: go in, because you have to be cautious and I haven't finished describing what you see.

Beat.

LOUISE: Alright, finish describing what I see.

Beat.

MARK: '– and there are glints of moonlight on the ramparts.'

LOUISE: Is that it?

MARK: Yes.

LOUISE: I go in.

MARK: You can't just go in.

LOUISE: Why not?

MARK: Because it might be dangerous.

LOUISE: Is it dangerous?

MARK: That's what you have to find out.

LOUISE: Can you just fucking tell me?

MARK: No, because you have to

LOUISE: This is shit.

MARK: It's not shit.

It's not shit, Louise.

You have to figure out whether it's dangerous from what I tell you, from my description, from

LOUISE: Alright.

MARK: from what I've said

LOUISE: Alright, alright!

Can I ask the pixie?

MARK: (*Beat.*) She's an elf. There are no pixies in this game. Pixies are from children's fairy stories and this is not –

LOUISE: Can I ask the elf?

MARK: You can ask the elf.

Pause.

LOUISE: Alright then.

MARK: What?

LOUISE: I ask the fucking elf!

MARK: What, what do you ask her, what do you –

LOUISE: I turn to the elf and say 'Is it dangerous?'

MARK: She says 'I don't now'

LOUISE: Fucking hell.

MARK: but she says 'It wouldn't be too wise to walk into that light.'

LOUISE: What does that mean?

MARK: Look Louise, I can't tell you every –

LOUISE: Give me the description again.

Beat.

MARK: 'You come out of the forest and suddenly the Keep is in front of you, like a ragged and ancient tooth on the hillside, jutting up into the night sky. It's covered in vines and ivy and bits of it are crumbling and the ancient path wends up to the portcullis. On either side of the portcullis are two forbidding statues of warriors, suggesting the ancient civilisation that once inhabited the keep, long since past. An eerie glow exudes from these statues bathing the entrance in a dull light and there are glints of moonlight on the ramparts.'

Beat.

LOUISE: This is what you used to dream about? Being in a caravan with this? A dwarf and a pixie and a tower shaped like a tooth?

Pause.

MARK: She's an elf. She's an elf and you know she's an elf. You're just saying pixie because you want to sabotage the game. If you're not going to play it properly then you shouldn't –

LOUISE: You're starving me into playing it!

MARK: To help you, to look after you!

LOUISE: To look after me?

MARK: You say 'Yeah, I'll play' but you can't just, just accept it and play, you have to call an elf a pixie just to remind me that you're better than me.

LOUISE: Who the fuck –?

You're looking after me?

MARK: Are you going to play it properly?

Beat.

LOUISE: You're looking after me, Mark?

MARK: Louise –

LOUISE: Let's play.

Beat.

MARK: Properly?

LOUISE: Let's play.

MARK: Louise. I want to get on.

Beat.

LOUISE: Alright. Give me the description again.

MARK: 'You come out of the forest and suddenly the Keep is in front of you, like a ragged and ancient tooth on the hillside, jutting up into the night sky. It's covered in vines and ivy and bits of it are crumbling and the ancient path wends up to the portcullis. On either side of the portcullis are two forbidding statues of warriors, suggesting the ancient civilisation that once inhabited the keep, long since past. An eerie glow exudes from these statues bathing the entrance in a dull light and there are glints of moonlight on the ramparts.'

LOUISE: I walk forward, out of the forest

MARK: I don't think that's

LOUISE: Can I do what I want?

MARK: Yes, you can, you can

LOUISE: I walk forward, out of the forest, very slowly,

MARK: Ariel hisses at you to, to come back –

LOUISE: very slowly, taking off my top

MARK: (*Beat.*) What?

LOUISE: I'm taking off my top and walking very slowly into the light.

MARK: That's

LOUISE: I pull my top over my head to reveal my bra.

MARK: They wouldn't've had

LOUISE: My undergarments, I pull my top over my head

MARK: That's just stupid, Louise.

LOUISE: to reveal my undergarments, and still I walk forward

MARK: That's –

LOUISE: And still I walk forward.

MARK: (*Beat.*) The glints, you can see the glints moving on the rampart

LOUISE: I carry on walking and drop my top to the ground,

MARK: the glints are moving, Louise.

LOUISE: and I begin to undo my belt

MARK: Louise –

LOUISE: Oops; my skirt has fallen to the ground.

MARK: You hear a shout in orcish from the ramparts and you suddenly realise that the glints were glints on the metal of the weapons of a troop of orcs.

LOUISE: I walk forward very slowly into the light taking off my undergarments

MARK: Louise –

LOUISE: I pull it over my head, revealing my perfect elvish breasts

MARK: You're a dwarf.

LOUISE: revealing my perfect dwarfish breasts

MARK: (*Rolling a dice.*) An orc arrow whistles past you.

LOUISE: I'm naked now and I'm waving at the orcs

MARK: Right, Ariel runs forward to defend –

LOUISE: I hit her with my sword.

MARK: What?

LOUISE: In the face.

MARK: (*Rolling a dice.*) You've killed her.

LOUISE: I drop my sword and grab my tits

MARK: They start firing

LOUISE: and I wave my perfect elvish tits at them and

He suddenly scrumples up all the papers, throws them to the floor and turns to her. There is a fraction of a moment when violence seems possible. It passes.

MARK: If you want to call me a cunt just call me a cunt.

LOUISE: You're a cunt.

Pause. He sits down away from her. He pulls out an energy bar. Opens it. She watches.

Give me some of that.

He begins to eat. Slowly.

Mark.

Eats, taking his time.

You better give me some.

Nearly finished.

Mark!

Last bit.

You better give me some.

Raises it to his mouth.

I mean it, Mark, don't do that, because if you, if you do that, I mean it, because I'll really –

Puts it in his mouth. Chews. Swallows. She stares.

You fucking –

You fucking –

Pause. She stares, impotent. Walks away, furious. Calms.

Beat.

I remember now. I remember what I thought when I first met you.

Beat.

MARK: What?

LOUISE: Yeah. I just remembered.

MARK: Don't say something just to get at me.

LOUISE: No. This is true.

MARK: Yeah, but don't say something just to –

LOUISE: This is exactly what I thought.

MARK: Louise, don't because –

LOUISE: No, Mark, this is true.

Shall I tell you? Shall I tell you, Mark? Do you want to know?

Beat.

I thought 'Ahhh'.

Pause.

MARK: No, you didn't.

LOUISE: I thought 'Ahhh'.

MARK: I don't care.

You didn't think, you're just saying –

I don't care.

LOUISE: I thought 'Ahhh. Look at him. Ahhh.'

Pause.

MARK: I could really hurt you.

I could really hurt you.

Beat.

I could really hurt you.

Tens of thousands of corpses up there. People vaporised into shadows. No-one knows you're here. I could really hurt you. If I was a bad person.

* * *

LOUISE waking MARK, desperate.

LOUISE: Voices!

MARK: What?

LOUISE: Voices, Mark, I think I heard, outside there's

MARK: What, what is, where?

LOUISE: Mark?

MARK: What?

LOUISE: Out there, voices,

MARK: Voices?

LOUISE: Yes, I heard

MARK: (*Getting out of bed.*) No…

LOUISE: I think so

MARK: Are you sure?

LOUISE: Well, I think so, I think, no, I'm not sure but I mean I was

MARK: Were you sleeping?

LOUISE: I don't think so, I don't think –

MARK: Shh.

LOUISE: I heard

MARK: Shhhh, I want to listen.

They listen.

LOUISE: I heard

MARK: Shhhh!

LOUISE: Mark, maybe it's alright, maybe we can

MARK: Louise!

They listen.

MARK: There's nothing.

LOUISE: No.

Beat.

But I think there was, Mark.

MARK: Well...

LOUISE: I'm sure I wasn't

MARK: I mean, down here we can't hear

LOUISE: I know, I know, but maybe

MARK: four foot of earth, I mean

LOUISE: The voice, the sound, maybe the sound travelled down

MARK: What did the voice say?

LOUISE: (*Beat.*) It was a boy.

MARK: A boy?

LOUISE: Yeah. There were boys, they were talking about clubbing and

MARK: Clubbing?

LOUISE: Yes.

Yes, I –

I don't think I was sleeping, I mean...

I mean...

MARK: Clubbing?

LOUISE: Well... and a girl called Chimge [*pronounced Chim-gay*]

I know it sounds, but I'm sure, Mark, I think I was

Jesus, I mean.

MARK: It was a dream.

LOUISE: Was it?

MARK: Boys talking about clubbing and a girl called Chimge?

Beat.

171

LOUISE: Let's bang on the hatch.

MARK: What for?

LOUISE: Get their attention.

MARK: Who, there's no-one out there.

LOUISE: I know, but maybe, because if we could go out

MARK: Stay away from the hatch.

LOUISE: Mark

MARK: That is the most vulnerable part of the whole shelter, everywhere else, four feet of earth. Stay away from the hatch. Go to bed.

He begins to get into bed. She waits, still unsure. Suddenly she rushes to the hatch, begins banging on it.

LOUISE: HEY!

MARK: Louise!

LOUISE: HEY, IN HERE, HEY!

MARK: Stop!

LOUISE: HEY, HEY!

He drags her down.

MARK: What the fuck are you doing?

LOUISE: What if they're out there?

MARK: Who, who? Who the fuck is out there?

LOUISE: I know but

MARK: All that is out there is a blanket of nuclear fucking fallout, and if you open that hatch

LOUISE: I'm not talking about opening

MARK: you let in an avalanche of radioactive dust

LOUISE: I know, I'm sorry, but what if it I wasn't dreaming?

MARK: that will kill us, you mean what if there were boys sitting out there in that nuclear fallout chatting about clubbing and a girl called Chimge?

LOUISE: Well if you say it like that

MARK: Are you okay?

LOUISE: Am I okay?

MARK: Have you had any other, I mean have you heard anything else?

LOUISE: No

MARK: Noises or voices

LOUISE: No.

MARK: because −

Here, have some food.

Unchains box. Begins to get some food out.

LOUISE: What?

MARK: D'you want some, here, here look, I'm gonna give

LOUISE: Yes.

MARK: Here.

He offers her an energy bar. She takes it.

LOUISE: Thank you.

Begins eating before he can take it back. She stops. Stares at him.

MARK: What?

Pause.

What?

LOUISE: Why are you giving me food?

Beat.

MARK: Because…

LOUISE: What?

MARK: You're hungry, you need –

LOUISE: I've been hungry for the last four days, why now?

MARK: Because…

things, you're hearing, you're…

hallucinating.

LOUISE: Okay.

Pause.

Mark?

MARK: Yes?

LOUISE: Can I ask you something?

MARK: Yes.

LOUISE: And you not get angry?

MARK: Depends what you ask.

LOUISE: Will you promise?

MARK: No, because it depends what you –

LOUISE: What's out there?

MARK: What's out there?

LOUISE: Yes.

MARK: What d'you mean? Rubble and

LOUISE: Really?

MARK: fallout and, yes, really, bodies and you know, you know what's

LOUISE: I don't know.

MARK: out there?

LOUISE: I don't know what's out there. I haven't seen it.

Pause.

MARK: What? What are you –?

I mean are you saying –?

Louise?

Is that what you think of me?

Pause.

LOUISE: No.

But is it true?

Beat. He snatches the energy bar out of her hand.

MARK: You fucking cunt.

LOUISE: Sorry

MARK: You fucking cunt, you fucking, fucking

LOUISE: sorry, look I'm sorry, but

MARK: after everything, everything I've

LOUISE: don't get all, because I'm just

MARK: done, everything, saving your, saving your fucking life, Louise!

He grabs her by the neck. Stares at her.

LOUISE: Mark, let go!

He doesn't.

Mark, let go!

He doesn't. She tries prying his hand away, but it's no good.

Let fucking go.

She Struggles more. Gives up.

Alright, I'm sorry, okay? I'm sorry, I'm really fucking sorry, only I had to, I mean I haven't seen, I'm just taking your –

Will you let go, please?

Mark, please?

Please!

He lets her go. Pause. They stare at each other. Suddenly she pushes him and heads for the hatch. He grabs her, throws her to the floor, twists her arm behind her back causing her to scream in pain and frustration. Grabs the chain.

What? What do you what?

Chains her ankle.

Alright, look you've made your point, I'm sorry, I'm really fucking sorry, now please let go.

Mark, please!

MARK: I'm not having you open that hatch!

Chains her to the bunk, gets off. She recoils.

This is what you're making me do. This is what you are making me do to you to help you. To help you Louise, this is what I have to do to you to help you. No more nice!

LOUISE: Mark –

MARK: Why are you doing this to me?

End

She sits chained to her bunk, he sits at the table, wanking, talking to himself, muttering inaudible stuff. He stares deliberately at her, though it is as if she is not there. This goes on for some time. He comes. Cleans himself with the Dungeons and Dragons papers. Sits there panting, cock in hand. He looks up at her as if noticing her for the first time. Looks down. Begins to cry. Starts playing with himself. Gets hard. Starts wanking again, staring at her, still crying. She glares at nothing.

* * *

MARK wakes up to find that LOUISE has a knife to his throat. It is the knife that he cut the apple with, a kitchen or hunting knife about six to eight inches long.

Pause. She motions him out of the bed with the knife. He gets out of the bed. He is wearing only his underpants. They stand there, the knife to his throat. She indicates that he should sit on the floor. He does so. Pause. She is unsure of what to do next.

MARK: We could have a conversation –

Beat.

We could –

God. This has gone a bit, you know, far and, hasn't it? And – I mean we're friendly, and friends and all this…

We could have a conversation, a talk and –

LOUISE: Key.

Finds his trousers, Holds out the key.

Do it.

He undoes the padlock, leaving the key in it, takes off the chain.

Food.

He goes to the chest, opens it. Pulls out a can of chilli, opens it, gives it to her. She eats, staring at him.

Cold.

Pause.

Said I'm cold.

He sets up the stove, turns it on. She eats, watching him. Finishes.

Water.

He passes her the water. She drinks. Lots.

Turn round.

Does so.

Sit on your hands.

Does so.

Look down. Close your eyes.

Does so.

She puts the radio on.

LOUISE: That stays on, alright.

She takes off her top, keeping her bra on. Washes herself, dries herself, puts her top back on. Stands up. Looks at him. Stands close to him.

MARK: There's not much left, we have to be –

LOUISE: Don't look at me!

He looks down.

Cunt.

Stupid cunt.

She washes. Gets up. Considers.

Stand up.

He does so.

Close your eyes.

Does so.

Put your arms out.

Does so.

Up.

Does so.

Stand on one leg.

Does so.

Open your eyes.

Does so.

Sit.

Does so. She goes over to him.

I could really hurt you.

Beat.

I could really hurt you.

I could really hurt you.

MARK: Alright, I think this has –

LOUISE: Get your cock out.

MARK: What?

LOUISE: Get your cock out.

MARK: No.

    Beat.

No. No, Louise.

Pause. He gets his cock out. She passes him some water.

LOUISE: Wash it.

Washes it. She throws him a towel.

Dry it.

He dries it. She goes over to him. Holds his cock. He tries not to look scared. She places the blade of the knife under his cock. Pause.

LOUISE: What's up there?

MARK: What?

LOUISE: Answer!

MARK: Fallout, rubble –

LOUISE: What about the boys?

MARK: What boys?

LOUISE: The boys I heard, what about –

MARK: A dream –

LOUISE: I'm gonna cut your cock off.

MARK: Please don't.

LOUISE: Gonna cut it off and watch.

MARK: Please, please don't –

LOUISE: Tell me!

MARK: I have!

LOUISE: Is that the truth?

MARK: It's the truth, it's true it's –

LOUISE: Is it?

MARK: Yes, yes, please, don't, please, please…

Beat. He is crying.

Please! Please don't!

She moves away. Stares at him. Waits.

LOUISE: Stop crying.

Stop fucking crying.

Looks at the hatch. At him. Thinks.

Put the chain on.

He doesn't move.

Put the chain on.

MARK: No.

LOUISE: Put –

MARK: Alright, Look, Louise; please don't make me put the chain on.

LOUISE: Put it on.

MARK: I won't do anything, please.

LOUISE: Put it on.

MARK: I'll be good, honestly, I won't –

LOUISE: Put it on.

MARK: I don't want to wear –

LOUISE: Put. It. On.

Pause. He puts the chain around his neck. Picks up the padlock.

MARK: Think the key's stuck

LOUISE: Put it on

MARK: I think it's jammed or

LOUISE: It's not jammed

MARK: no, hang on

LOUISE: don't

MARK: I'm just gonna

Breaks key under his foot.

LOUISE: Don't –

MARK: Broke.

Sorry. It… it just

broke.

She stare at him, furious.

LOUISE: I'll stab you…

She goes for him. He dodges the blow, but she comes at him again. Unable to get away he cowers on the floor, covering his head with his hands.

MARK: Sorry, sorry. Sorry, sorry, sorry, sorry…

Please?

Louise, it's Mark, it's Mark!

She stops. Moves back, shaken.

Thank you.

Thank you.

Pause.

Shitter.

* * *

LOUISE is sitting over the stove, which has a pot on it. She pokes at the contents of the pot on it with her knife. The stove is unlit. She is wrapped in a blanket, he is not, shivering. MARK watches her. The radio spews static.

MARK: …and there was the time when your car broke down. D'you remember when your car broke down? We were in the Mitre and you were driving because you were off

up to see your dad and you were sitting next to me, in the
beer garden and we were squashed because there was a lot
of us and you were squashed up against me, but it wasn't
like that, but it was beautiful, and I was there with Pete
and he was being alright, he wasn't being, Pete was being
alright, for once, and the sun was going down and I was
wondering what you were thinking. I was thinking 'What
is she thinking?' And I looked up and there was a star in
the red, this bright star, and I thought that the world would
be a perfect world if I could talk just to you. And then I
thought maybe we were. Maybe on some level our souls
were communicating, and I saw these beings of light, you
know, the real us, not this corporeal, entwining around
each other. And when you went, it was like dying and
going down the tunnel and then being ripped back into this
world by a defibrillator.

And then you came back. You just suddenly appeared and
I heard myself saying 'You can stay at mine' and you said
'Can I?' and I said. 'Yeah. Yeah, of course.' And it was like
the world had changed and every thing on the planet was
possible. It was a new world.

But you stayed with Mandy.

Silence. She tries some rice. Spits it out.

I told you.

LOUISE: Shut up.

MARK: I told you, it's inedible. It won't work. You need gas to
cook rice.

LOUISE: I'm soaking it.

MARK: You can't soak it. It'll be sludge. You're cooking sludge.

LOUISE: Don't speak.

MARK: There's days to go. Two, three days maybe.

LOUISE: Can last two days

MARK: Look at you. Jesus Christ, look at you, at what you've become.

LOUISE: Look at you.

MARK: Look at you. You can't live on rice. Uncooked rice.

LOUISE: Shut your mouth.

MARK: Okay, I'll shut up, I'll just shut up then, shall I.

Beat. She begins to scoop out the rice, try and make it into balls.

D'you remember softball? Softball? D'you remember softball? I remember softball. Everyone there, the whole company and I remember sitting under that tree with you, do you remember the tree, it was like a big, it was a big, and I wish I knew what type of tree it was, that's something I always mean to do is learn the names of trees, maybe some plants, I dunno, but we sat under that tree and this was probably only for, no more than, what? fifteen minutes? twenty at the most? and yes there was drink and yes you'd had a few and yes I'd been doing very well, a home run and I'd caught that, their first batter, I'd caught her out and yes, yes alright, all these things, yes, but we talked, we talked, Louise. D'you remember? We really talked. D'you remember? do you Louise? we talked about the existence of life on other planets. And I was saying how they'd discovered methane on Mars and that this was probably the result of microbes producing the methane, d'you remember? and we talked about what happens if we discover life on the first planet we go to considering there's billions of galaxies, two hundred million stars in ours alone, that it would mean the universe was teeming with life, and it was like we were explorers, d'you remember? it was like we were explorers in ideas, it was like we were the first humans in an alien landscape and I could almost feel the tree growing under our backs and I turned to you and said 'Aren't we lucky.' And you said 'Yes.' 'Yes' you said. And 'I thought I love this woman, this woman, I love –'

The radio suddenly goes silent. Pause. LOUISE goes over to it.

No radio.

LOUISE: Shut up.

She picks it up. Fiddles with it, but it is dead.

MARK: Batteries. No radio.

LOUISE: Shut. Up.

MARK: You can't last three days.

LOUISE: Can

MARK: No food, no radio.

LOUISE: So?

MARK: I can forgive you.

LOUISE: Shut up.

MARK: Look what you're doing to us. You can't last.

LOUISE: Can.

MARK: Can't.

LOUISE: Can.

MARK: Can't.

LOUISE: Can.

MARK: Can't, Louise, can't.

She goes back to the stove, but realising that the rice is useless he has nothing to do. Pause.

Then there was the fire drill. D'you remember that time they did the fire drill? There was the fire drill, d'you remember the fire drill, Louise? They called the fire drill and we all had to gather outside Tesco's and we started joking that this'd be a good time for the weekly shop, d'you remember that? I remember that, and there was the time when a dog came into the building, d'you remember when a dog came into the building? a stray dog and everyone stopped work and

She puts her hands over her ears.

watched, because I mean there was a dog in the building and we were saying, d'you remember, we were saying that Tony was probably going to ask it if it wanted to be a line manager and Tony was a little miffed at that and…

*   *   *

MARK lies on his bunk fast asleep. LOUISE sits at the table, knife in hand, but her head is nodding. She almost falls asleep but at the last minute she wakes. Panics, looks at MARK, but he is still asleep. She shakes her head, tries to rub the sleep from her eyes. She tries to stay awake but soon her head is nodding again. This time she nearly drops the knife. She gets up, walks around. Goes over to look at MARK, see if he's really asleep. She goes to the hatch. Goes and sits on the cold floor. Changes position, keeping an eye on MARK. Sits kneeling on the floor so that she can't sleep. Dozes out. Shakes her head. Gets up, goes over to MARK again, but he is still fast asleep. Goes back to her kneeling position on the floor. Her head nods.

Lower. Lower.

Lower.

She is asleep.

The hand with the knife is in her lap.

She sleeps. Somehow this position has beome tenable.

She sleeps.

She sleeps.

MARK gets up silently and quickly, in one move, goes straight to her and grabs the knife from her hand. She recoils, instantly awake. He stands there in his underpants holding the knife. She backs away. They stare at each other. He has the knife at arm's length, furious. Long pause. He sags. Tries not to cry. She stares. The arm with the knife lowers, slowly. He is crying now, quietly, head bowed. She stares at him. Pause. He shuffles towards her, head lowered.

She is frozen. He moves into her, puts his arms around her, crying, buries his face in her neck. She stands. They stay like that for a while. Slowly, she raises her arms, returning the hug, but.

LOUISE: There, there

there, there.

They hug, both needing it.

They hug.

He begins to kiss her neck. She tries to pull away but he is clutching her hard.

Mark?

Mark?

His hand is on her breasts, in her hair, while he kisses her face through his tears. She struggles now, pushing hard at him. He lifts the knife to her neck and she freezes. He kisses her face, her mouth, still crying but pushing his groin up into her, against her.

She doesn't move.

Mark?

MARK: My love. My darling.

LOUISE: Mark?

MARK: My beautiful darling, my beautiful Louise.

LOUISE: Mark?

His hands are inside her clothes.

Mark, don't –

He pushes the knife against her neck and she freezes.

MARK: My beautiful darling, my beautiful Louise.

He begins to undo her trousers, yanks them down. He is still crying. He forces her to the ground. He pulls off her trousers and knickers, kissing her stomach

My beautiful Louise, beautiful, beautiful

He performs oral sex on her, the knife now held directly above her stomach, the tip of the blade touching her skin. She stares at him. He comes back up, knife to her throat.

LOUISE: Don't

MARK: I love you.

LOUISE: Don't

MARK: My beautiful

LOUISE: Don't

MARK: Louise

He penetrates her. He moves with increasing desperation, still crying, occasionally saying 'my beautiful Louise'. She waits for him to finish.

* * *

MARK sits wrapped in a blanket and his thoughts. LOUISE is also wrapped in a blanket.

MARK: Does it –

Does it hurt, or…

She takes a sheet of Dungeons and Dragons paper and lays it on the floor.

I'm sorry. I didn't mean to –

It was sort of an accident. I'm not that sort of –

Jesus Christ. Oh my God. (*Winces.*) Fuck. Oh fuck.

She sprinkles rice onto the sheet. It is as if he isn't there. She begins to roll the gas canister over the rice to crush it.

Oh my God. I'm sorry. Why can't you just –

Why can't you just like me? Please. Why won't you like me, Louise?

LOUISE: Coz you're a cunt.

He stares at her. The gas cylinder is not working. She takes two pieces of Dungeons and Dragons paper, lays them on the sheet and places a grain of rice onto one. She lifts the gas cylinder and brings the corner of it down onto the grain of rice. She pours the resultant powder into the other sheet of paper. She repeats the process.

MARK: What are you doing?

LOUISE: Making rice flour.

MARK: Why?

LOUISE: I tried eating it whole and I shat it all out.

MARK: I do think there should be tax on airline fuels.

Beat.

I wanted to say sorry. That's what I wanted to do, when I came out of the pub after you. D'you remember? I wanted to say, I wanted to say sorry. Because when you said that thing about tax on airline fuel and cheap holidays and things I think I sounded a bit arsey. But I didn't mean to. Because I agree. It's the third biggest, you know, pollutant and, I agree, really, so, but I was, we all like a cheap holiday and its one thing to say, isn't it, but doing is, but I wasn't being arsey. It came out wrong.

Beat.

LOUISE: What?

MARK: In the pub.

LOUISE: Pub?

MARK: After the pub. I came out of the pub after and –

Remember?

Pause. She doesn't. She goes back to the rice. She pounds on.

MARK: I'm going to kill myself.

LOUISE: Where?

MARK: Over here.

LOUISE: How?

MARK: I'm going to stab myself in the neck with this knife.

LOUISE: Put a sheet down.

MARK: Okay.

He gets up, goes to his bed, grabs a sheet and brings it over to the table. She continues pounding the rice, a grain at a time. He looks at the table, figuring out where he will fall. He sits down in position to get a better idea of it. Experiments with the knife. Discovers that the best way may be to rest the butt of the knife on the table and push his throat onto the blade. Satisfied he puts the knife down, gets up and lays the blanket on the table. On second thoughts he pushes the edges of the blanket into walls, forming a pool. He sits down, puts the butt of the knife against the table, holds it with both hands and readies his neck. Pause. She pounds on. He stops.

MARK: Which side is the jugular on?

LOUISE: Right.

She pounds. He adjusts the knife so that it will go through the right side of his neck. Readies himself. Stops. Pause.

MARK: You'll die without me.

LOUISE: So.

MARK: Let's go together.

LOUISE: No.

She pounds. Suddenly he comes at her with the knife, but she uses the canister as a weapon and hits him on the elbow. He shouts at the pain but is shocked. They stare at each other, weapons at the ready.

No.

MARK: Yes.

LOUISE: No.

MARK: Yes.

LOUISE: No.

MARK: Did I do something wrong? I mean is there a moment when I could have done something different and you would've felt something different towards me?

LOUISE: No.

MARK: I fucking love you!

LOUISE: So?

MARK: Doesn't that mean anything to you?

LOUISE: No.

MARK: Not nothing?

LOUISE: No.

MARK: I'm going to fucking kill you! I'm going to fucking kill you and then kill myself if you don't love me.

LOUISE: Go on, then.

MARK: I mean it!

LOUISE: Go on. I'll smash your brains out with this.

MARK: I'll win. You know I'll win.

LOUISE: I don't care.

MARK: Look at you. Look at what you're like now.

LOUISE: So?

MARK: I'm going to kill you, Louise. Just say you fucking love me!

LOUISE: No.

He rushes her. She swings the canister, but he dodges the blow. She tries again, but it is too heavy to use as a weapon, and he manages to tear it out of her grasp. He grabs her by the throat, knife pulled back to stab her.

MARK: Say it!

LOUISE: No.

MARK: Please!

LOUISE: No.

MARK: Louise!

Pulls the knife back to stab. Suddenly there is banging on the hatch. They stop. Listen. More banging, deliberate. They stare at each other. Pause.

The wheel starts to turn.

Say it.

Pause. The hatch opens, light floods in.

Say it, Louise.

LOUISE: No.

MARK: Please.

LOUISE: No.

MARK: Please.

LOUISE: No.

MARK: Please.

LOUISE: No.

After the End

Private visiting room in a prison. MARK sits at the table. There is a GUARD by the back wall. LOUISE enters, MARK stands. She is dressed up, but standing by the door, looking awkward, not quite knowing what to do. This goes on for some time. She seems to be waiting for the GUARD to say something, but he is silent.

MARK: You…

You can just sit if you want.

She sits. He sits.

LOUISE: Hello.

MARK: Hello.

Beat.

You look –

Beat.

LOUISE: It smells in here.

MARK: Does it?

LOUISE: Yeah. Cleaning stuff, cheap cleaning stuff. I went to the toilet and washed my hands and it reminded me of this cheap hotel I stayed in in Turkey. I've never smelt that anywhere else. Straight back there. Five years. But it's like if I sniff my hands and try and be back there I can't. You know, it's like I can't

MARK: I know

LOUISE: catch it

MARK: yeah, yeah I know

LOUISE: with a memory or something

MARK: that's funny with smells isn't it.

I don't notice that there's a smell, though.

Long pause.

LOUISE: What's it like in here?

MARK: Ah, you know.

Beat.

LOUISE: No, what?

MARK: Pretty shit.

It's prison.

LOUISE: My solicitor said I shouldn't come.

MARK: Yeah?

LOUISE: She was dead against it.

MARK: My counsellor thought it was a good idea.

LOUISE: She thought it might compromise the case.

MARK: I don't think it would –

LOUISE: Are you getting counselling?

MARK: Yeah, I'm –

LOUISE: You're not a solicitor so you wouldn't know.

MARK: No.

LOUISE: Is it helping?

Is it helping you?

MARK: I think so.

Yes.

Maybe.

It helps me come to terms with

what I –

LOUISE: I fucked Francis.

Beat.

I was getting counselling. I stopped it. Didn't need it.
I'm fine. She was very good but I felt sorry for her. She
believed in forming a bond through empathy. Empathy as
a two-way channel. So I would tell her what it felt like to
find out that all your friends and your family and everyone
you know had been incinerated in a nuclear attack and
she'd tell me about missing out on sports day because her
mother didn't believe in competitive sports. Embarrassing.
Stopped going. Spare us both.

MARK: How's Francis?

LOUISE: He's good. He's going out with Sarah.

MARK: Is he?

LOUISE: Yeah.

MARK: Really?

LOUISE: Yeah.

MARK: Sarah?

LOUISE: Yeah.

Beat.

MARK: When did that happen?

LOUISE: That night we were all in the pub. Funny, eh. Then
they sort of messed around for a month or so, you know,
not sure sort of thing, but now…

Beat.

I don't think he wanted to fuck me. I think he was just
being polite. I just thought it might help me, you know,
find out some stuff. I scared the shit out of him actually.
He looked terrified. I never really liked him that much. It
just sort of became this thing, you know. You kept fucking
talking about it.

Beat.

I had a hard time adjusting. First month or so. But I'm fine now.

MARK: Why did you come here?

LOUISE: How big is your cell?

MARK: Ten by eight.

LOUISE: Are there bars on the windows?

MARK: No, glass it's sort of –

LOUISE: D'you share it?

MARK: No, I'm not very, they're worried that the others –

LOUISE: What's the food like?

MARK: It – it's not too bad.

LOUISE: Really?

MARK: Yeah, no, it's not great, but…

LOUISE: It's not too bad, though?

MARK: No, it's alright.

LOUISE: I thought 'I'll go in and ask him to kill himself'.

Beat.

I'm sitting there at home, last night, with this, with this cat in my lap and I thought 'I'll go in there and I'll ask him to kill himself. That's what I'll do.' So I called my solicitor this morning and told her that I was going in after all and I called the prison service and they were very good, I thought it might take weeks, but they sorted out an appointment for today, which is quick, isn't it.

No answer.

I thought 'I'll go in, I'll ask him to kill himself and he'll do it. He'll do what I ask. Because he was going to kill both

197

of us anyway. No matter what his solicitor says, I know. I know.'

What do you do in here?

D'you get bored?

Do you read?

No answer.

Do you get telly?

MARK: Yes.

LOUISE: Yes? That's good.

Pause.

I find telly one of the most difficult things. Or I did when I was finding it difficult to adjust. My reactions to it are completely inappropriate. I'm at my mum's watching the news and this suicide bombing comes on and I start laughing, because seventy-six dead and they're all so serious.

I'm much better now.

Buying food was hard at first because I just kept buying it. I'd take stuff to the counter, hand over the money and almost run out of the shop, like I was stealing or something. This one time I was at Sarah's, there was a bunch of us and I saw this tin opener on the counter and I just put it in my pocket, and when I turned round they were all pretending they hadn't seen it happen and I wanted to fucking punch them.

MARK: Louise –

LOUISE: Don't

say

my fucking

name.

Beat.

I figured out how to make it better though. I just try and work out who I was and I act that. I just act that. It's getting easier. They said there would be a period of adjustment. It's getting much easier. The difficult thing is remembering. I find it hard to remember. And when I do I feel, like,

grief.

MARK: I'm sorry.

LOUISE: Are you?

MARK: Yes.

LOUISE: Well. That's alright then.

Beat.

So you're getting counselling?

MARK: Yeah. Yes. I'm in group.

LOUISE: In group?

MARK: Yeah.

LOUISE: Do you like it in group?

MARK: Yeah. Yeah, I do.

LOUISE: That's good.

MARK: I want to apo –

LOUISE: I think a lot about what makes people do things. What makes us behave in certain ways, you know. Every night I been thinking about this. Trapped in whatever, behaviour, I dunno, cycles of violence or something and is it possible to break, these cycles, is it possible to break... And I'd be sitting there thinking about this and this cat, this gorgeous cat with no tail would come to my door, I'd have the back door open because the garden looks, and she'd be terrified at first, it looks beautiful it really does. So I bought some food for her and the first time she just sniffed at it and ran away, the moment I moved, you know, no sign of her for the rest of the night, and I'm thinking, reactions and responses, patterns, violence breeding violence, and the next night she's in a bit further and I'm looking at her tail thinking 'that's been cut off' and I don't think it was, I think she's a Manx, I think they're born without tails, and the next night she's further in and I'm beginning to get used to this, beginning to look forward to it. And the next night she's in and she's eating and from then on she's in every night; she's on my lap, she's following me around, she's waiting on the window ledge for me when I get home. And we sit there every night and I'm thinking behaviour and patterns and is it actually possible to break these patterns or whatever and she's eating and meowing to be let in. Every night. And one night she scratches me, out of the blue, cats, you know, just a vindictive cat-scratch, look:

Shows him.

see?

MARK: Yeah.

LOUISE: Just here.

MARK: Yeah.

Beat.

LOUISE: She knew she'd done wrong.

Took her three nights to get back into my lap. And I'm stroking her and thinking. Warm, delicate, you know. And I put my hands around her neck. And I squeeze. And I squeeze. Until her neck is about the thickness of a rope. And still I squeeze. And I'm sitting there – and this is last night – with this dead cat in my lap, and I thought I'd come in and see you.

And here I am.

Long pause.

I started the job.

MARK: Did you?

LOUISE: Yeah. A different one though. They gave my one
away. But they made a new one for me.

MARK: That's nice.

LOUISE: Yeah.

Only I'm not quite sure what I'm supposed to do and they
seem too embarrassed to tell me. I thought that it was
just going to be like that for the first week, but it's been a
month now and I don't seem any closer to knowing what
I'm supposed to be doing.

D'you know what? if I'm honest, I don't seem to be that
much closer to knowing what I'm supposed to be doing in
general.

Long pause.

MARK: When were you in Turkey?

LOUISE: Five years ago.

MARK: What was it like?

LOUISE: Why? are you thinking of going?

MARK: No I just –

LOUISE: Holidays, maybe?

MARK: I'm just asking.

LOUISE: Weekend away?

MARK: I'm just asking, Louise.

LOUISE: Why the fuck are you asking?

MARK: Because you won't let me say what I want to say.

LOUISE: It was very nice.

Beat.

It was very nice.

Beautiful actually. I wish I could smell that smell.

Beat.

I was going to bring you something but I didn't know whether I could.

MARK: Yeah, you can, you just give it to, there's a place out there you give it to them and fill in a form,

LOUISE: Right.

I thought grapes, but then I remembered that's a hospital.

Then I thought cake.

But then I remembered that's a joke.

MARK: Yeah.

LOUISE: Does anyone visit you?

MARK: No.

My mum. Once.

LOUISE: How is she?

MARK: Not too good.

How's yours.

LOUISE: Yeah.

I feel quite

alone.

MARK: So do I

Silence for a while.

Are you

Are you going to ask me?

LOUISE: What?

MARK: What you came here to ask me?

LOUISE: Pamukale. That was the place, in Turkey, that was the place, just remembered, we stayed, it was…

Haven't said that word in years, funny how…

how you don't lose a word, or…

Beat.

It was beautiful.

Pause.

Mark?

MARK: Yes?

Beat.

LOUISE: Do I look like me?

Beat.

MARK: Yes.

You do.

LOUISE: Do I?

MARK: Yes.

LOUISE: Honestly?

MARK: Yes, honestly.

LOUISE: Because I just need –

I was wondering, you know, I…

whether

I just need to know –

Honestly?

MARK: Yeah.

Pause.

LOUISE: I thought I did.

That's good.

That's good.

Silence.

Suddenly she gets up.

I think I'll go.

He gets up.

Better go.

MARK: Okay.

LOUISE: S'long way back.

MARK: Yeah, yeah.

Beat.

LOUISE: If I come again should I bring cigarettes?

MARK: I don't smoke.

LOUISE: Yeah, but you know; prison.

MARK: Just bring chocolate.

LOUISE: Right.

Over

LOVE AND MONEY

Characters

DAVID

MOTHER

FATHER

VAL

PAUL

JESS

1, 2, 3, 4 & 5

DUNCAN

DEBBIE

DOCTOR

Love and Money was first performed at The Studio, Royal Exchange Theatre on 27 October 2006, as part of a Young Vic / Royal Exchange co-production, with the following cast:

MOTHER / 2, Joanna Bacon

FATHER / 3 / DUNCAN, Paul Moriarty

DAVID / 5, John Kirk

JESS, Kellie Bright

VAL / 4 / DEBBIE, Claudie Blakley

PAUL / 1 / DOCTOR, Graeme Hawley

Direction Matthew Dunster

Design Anna Fleischle

Lighting Lucy Carter

Sound Ian Dickinson

Composer Olly Fox

ONE

DAVID: January eighteenth.

Hello

How are you? Just thought I'd email you to say hello.

Hello.

Beat.

Just wanted to say thanks for a really instructive couple of weeks and we hope that you learnt as much from us as we did from you. I can honestly say that despite our differing sales strategies (perhaps you found us a touch aggressive?) your customer service recommendations will have a very real impact on the way we do business. However, you will have to forgive me if I maintain a healthy British scepticism regarding your optical relaying systems. It'll never work!

He laughs. Beat.

Hope the Eurostar was okay. Are you missing our English food? If the pain gets too much my suggestion is have a look behind the fridge, find something brown, stick it in-between two slices of bread, et voila! The taste of England.

Beat.

And as well, I just wanted to say Hi. From me.

So hi.

I had a great time. And I don't just mean that (but that was great). So I thought I'd just email you coz... I just thought it was sort of...

Special.

There. Said it. Now I feel a twat.

David.

January nineteenth.

Bonjour David

Thank you for your mail and your beautiful gourmet. Yes, David, I discover a nice piece which sitting on my fridge waiting anticipatedly to become a Great British sandwich. Do you have any other recipes? Please: keep them.

I am happy to hear for you today. I ask to myself for this ten days 'Why does this cunt not email me (very British, yes?) Perhaps there is not a feeling that I thought?' But I forgive you because of your delicious sandwich, so thanks.

Optical relaying is the future. But please, what would a British know of the future?

Eurostar *c'est magnifique* as always. I get off at Gare du Nord and I see one child holding his mother's hand like an angel while other hand is making a steal of a candy from this stand outside a shop, while no-one see and I think of you, David, and I laugh, because you would laugh and I feel sad.

Yes, it was special. And the that (you have so many words for fucking in English, is this another?) was beautiful.

Write me again you Bastard Piece of English Shit.

Love

Sandrine.

January twentieth.

Dear Sandrine

Sorry I didn't write. I just thought, you know. I don't know, I thought maybe you might not want to write so I delayed or maybe I thought you would think I was a twat if I wrote you too soon. So there you are, now I do look like a twat. Now you think I'm a twat. But I did want to write to you.

Aren't men stupid?

Your description of the child stealing the candy was beautiful. Made me feel very sad that I wasn't there with you to laugh.

Pause. He thinks.

We had a funny thing here today. You remember that deal that Liam closed with Lanstowers? You must remember because he stood on my desk and did a dance (fat wanker)? Well it turns out that he was talking to the owner's thirteen year old daughter.

He laughs. Beat.

So it was really funny.

Beat.

David.

January twentieth. Same day.

Hello David

No, it is not men that are stupid. It is you that are stupid. Why do you say you are twat? And why do you tell me of this stupid story about this fat wanker and his sales of high speed access? Perhaps you believe I am interested so much to the instalment of telephonic lines that I am waiting with an anticipation to see what will happen next? I ask of myself 'is this the same man who told me my hair was smelled of the future and my eyes were hope?' I forgive you, of course, because you are British and a twat, but please, you can talk me of this bullshit of the telecommunications or you can talk me of how you feel, you cannot do both.

Bisses, Sandrine.

January twenty-first.

Okay.

How I feel.

Beat.

I feel confused. I feel happy. I feel frightened. I feel horny.
I feel desperate, I feel worthless because I'm not getting a
pay upgrade this year, I feel angry because I wrote such a
stupid thing to you and I feel inspired because you didn't
let me get away with it. I feel honest, you make me feel

honest and

I feel

Beat.

I feel like I'm betraying

the

memory

of my wife. Or something. I dunno.

Pause.

There. You wanted to know.

January twenty-first. Same day.

David, this is more to the point than telling of fat Liam's
internet access, no? I am glad you are feeling horny.
Happy and inspired is also good, but the rest is shit. David,
a year is a long time. Twelve months aggressive selling of
telecommunications is enough penance, yes?

Tell me of your wife.

January twenty-first. Same day.

Beat.

No, I don't think that would be

right.

January twenty-first. Same day.

Why?

January twenty-first. Same day.

Beat.

I

trust you, Sandrine. And I like you. I live this life here
where everything is measured in pay grades and pension
schemes and sales targets and people like Liam laugh when
your orders are cancelled and you are scared of losing your
job. And you

Beat.

I used to be a teacher, I…

Beat.

You

are outside of this. You are beautiful and outside of this and
you inspire me and you make me believe in things

that maybe it's not a good idea for me to believe in.

January twenty-first. Same day.

Tell me of your wife.

January twenty-first. Same day.

You asked me to tell you how I feel. I feel scared to tell you about my wife because perhaps if I do you will not email me again and I will be alone with Liam and his fibre optic cabling.

January twenty-first. Same day.

Tell me of your wife.

January twenty-first. Same day.

Sandrine.

Beat.

My wife –

Jess

killed herself.

I do not want to tell you of my wife.

Pause.

January twenty-first. Same day.

Tell me of your wife.

January twenty-first. Same day.

Tell me of your wife.

January twenty-first. Same day.

Tell me of your wife.

What? You think perhaps I take this information and make a book? You think I ask you to make some laugh, like this fat wanker? I kissed your tears. This was a taste of salt and now I taste salt thinking of your body.

Tell me of your wife. This is just a jump to make, yes? Trust please.

Pause.

January twenty-second. Nothing.

January twenty-third.

Okay.

I came home and she was lying on the bed and she'd taken –

Pause.

I'd been test driving this Audi. It was silver. It had ABS breaking, climate control, satellite navigation and roll bar as standard. It had these little push out trays for your drinks and things. It was a lovely car. I loved it. It really held the road

Beat.

well, and the thing was the bloke who's doing the test drive, you could just tell he was thinking 'you fucking waste of my time'. But the thing was I could afford it, but

Beat.

It felt so good that car. It felt like I'd earned that car, after the things I'd been through, the things I'd

done

it felt like that car was my right.

But we had debts, big debts. My wife had debts.

You see, he could see that I couldn't afford the car. Do you understand? It was visible on me. He could see it on me.

Pause.

So when I came home and saw her lying there I thought

I'll be able to afford the car now.

Beat.

You don't have to email back.

January twenty-third. Same day.

Why would I not to email you back? British twat. You are so honest and beautiful. You think I hate honesty? You think I hate beauty? I do not live in a Disney. And I do not say 'Oh please, this was some shock because you wife was dead'. This is real world, yes? I am real woman, yes? I go to find some salt to kiss so I can be with you.

January twenty-third. Same day.

My wife wasn't dead.

Beat.

I thought she was dead. At first. But she wasn't.

I thought that seventy thousand pounds worth of debt had just

died, but…

Beat.

She'd taken thirty to forty Xanax. I touched her skin and I realised she was still alive. Hardly breathing.

The debt was crushing us, it was...

Beat.

I sat down.

I waited. Ten minutes. Twenty minutes. Half hour. Forty-five minutes. She's still alive.

I waited.

January twenty-third. Same day.

Beat.

David, this is a strong thing you tell me. I have to think of this, yes?

January twenty-third. Same day.

I looked it up on the internet. While she was there, dying. About an hour I'd waited. She hadn't drunk any alcohol, you see.

January twenty-third. Same day.

Please, David, this is a very strong to me. Forgive me, please, but I must ask of you calling an ambulance?

January twenty-third. Same day.

You just feel crushed. I understood what she was doing. Then I'm thinking 'The car's going. I can see the Audi going.'

January twenty-third. Same day.

David, please. This is a hard and real for me. Please.

January twenty-third. Same day.

So I went downstairs. Went out. Got in the Micra. Drove to the shop. Came back with a bottle of Smirnoff.

Started feeding it to her, but it's going everywhere. So I get this straw and I tape it to the bottle with plumber's tape so it's all waterproof. And I put butter on the other end so that it doesn't scratch. And I slip it into her throat. And I start pouring. Get about a third of it in, she starts coughing and I'm scared and I get rid of the straw and tape because she's struggling and I think, marks, you know, marks in her throat. So I go back to pouring. And it's hard, it's very hard and

her

eyes

open.

And they look at me. With the bottle.

Really unfocused. But they knew. They look at me with the bottle.

Beat.

And I managed to feed her about another quarter. Her eyes looking at mine.

Looking into mine.

Looking into mine.

Beat.

No more emails that day.

January twenty-fourth. No emails.

January twenty-fifth. No emails.

January twenty-sixth. No emails.
Beat.

January twenty-seventh.
Sandrine?
Are you there?
I just wanted to say
hi.
Beat.

January twenty-eighth. No emails.

January twenty-ninth. No emails.

Etc. Etc.

Etc.

TWO

FATHER: So when we see the name

MOTHER: Keriakous

FATHER: Elena Keriakous

MOTHER: We're thinking

FATHER: On the grave next to our daughter's grave

MOTHER: we're thinking

FATHER: on the wooden cross, fresh grave, so a cross first

MOTHER: Jesus Christ

FATHER: Jesus Christ, what is coming – you put a cross down first then once the grave has had time to settle, once it's stable you're ready for the headstone

MOTHER: we're thinking, Jesus Christ

FATHER: that way the headstone doesn't

MOTHER: what is coming next

FATHER: shift – what is going to replace that cross?

MOTHER: What monument, what skyscraper is going to tower over our daughter

FATHER: D'you see?

MOTHER: Greek.

FATHER: The Greeks are very

MOTHER: flash

FATHER: ostentatious with their dead, not flash, no

MOTHER: great black stone, gold inlay, columns pillars, vulgar

FATHER: it's their culture, no not vulgar

MOTHER: crosses, photographic reproductions in stone of the deceased

FATHER: they're very respectful of their

MOTHER: and he was there every day, wasn't he

FATHER: every day he was there

MOTHER: Eighty if he was a day

FATHER: every day, she had a husband that would come every day and whilst I don't expect, you know, obviously people are busy, but this old Greek woman had a husband who would visit every day, while our daughter –

MOTHER: Everyone said at the wedding that it felt like we were intruders, but in a good way, it felt like there were two people in the room celebrating something sacred and the rest of us were just onlookers. Everyone said that. People were stunned by their love.

FATHER: Well, weddings…

Beat.

MOTHER: And our daughter's headstone is going down

FATHER: the grave's settled you see, it's had time, eighteen

MOTHER: nineteen

FATHER: yes, yes, nineteen months and it's, you know, it's a nice enough

MOTHER: white stone, black lettering, very

FATHER: Three thousand eight hundred pounds.

MOTHER: elegant, don't say how much!

FATHER: plus VAT.

MOTHER: don't say plus VAT!

FATHER: I'm just saying.

MOTHER: I mean for Christ's sake

FATHER: Seventeen-point-five per cent on three thousand eight hundred is a sizable

MOTHER: Well, don't say it all over again!

FATHER: I'm just saying, I'm just giving context and I mean it's two thousand five hundred pounds for the plot alone for the space, for the dirt that you put your daughter inside

MOTHER: We're not rich

FATHER: We once were

MOTHER: We were never rich

FATHER: Early eighties, eight-bedroom house

MOTHER: everyone in the early eighties, but if you haven't got the killer instinct

FATHER: what does that mean?

MOTHER: you've said it yourself

FATHER: yes, but now you're saying it

MOTHER: broke her heart moving from that house

FATHER: what are you saying now?

MOTHER: I'm just giving context, wept from her soul, never the same again

FATHER: that's just not

MOTHER: and all the time we're seeing this plot

FATHER: that's just not

MOTHER: thinking 'what's coming here?'

FATHER: no, don't distract, because that's just not

MOTHER: and he's bought the plot next to it

FATHER: that's

MOTHER: didn't he, he's bought the plot next to it, so that's more money

FATHER: well, two thousand five hundred, but

MOTHER: and he's fenced both in together, six inch picket fence

FATHER: another two and a half grand, but

MOTHER: and he's put a bench in it, didn't he,

FATHER: nice one too, expensive

MOTHER: like a park bench

FATHER: Yes, like a park bench

MOTHER: which he'd come and sit on every day

FATHER: and we would nod to him, we were friendly

MOTHER: but we're thinking

FATHER: what the hell is coming next? what's going on in that little balding head

MOTHER: and does he know

FATHER: does he know

MOTHER: how our daughter died

FATHER: and is he judging us

MOTHER: he's not judging us

FATHER: because we would've, if she'd come to us we'd've, wouldn't we would've helped, I mean we're not

MOTHER: Don't say rich.

FATHER: rich

MOTHER: Don't keep going on about

FATHER: If she'd have had a husband who loved

MOTHER: She did have a husband who

223

FATHER: If she'd've come to us

MOTHER: She did come to us

FATHER: yes, but if she'd've asked for

MOTHER: She did ask for help

FATHER: yes, but really meant it, if she'd've

MOTHER: She did really mean it!

Beat.

FATHER: And then it starts

MOTHER: Yes

FATHER: Huge black base

MOTHER: Yes

FATHER: Huge

MOTHER: Yes

FATHER: and we're thinking

MOTHER: Here we go

FATHER: here we effing go

MOTHER: and it's

FATHER: ridiculous

MOTHER: over the top

FATHER: I mean it's a temple

MOTHER: I mean he's practically building a temple on his wife's grave

FATHER: I mean and what does that say about us

MOTHER: I mean there's columns, golden filigree

FATHER: I mean what does that say about our love for

MOTHER: I mean four foot statues of the Madonna?

FATHER: we're watching this, we're seeing this go up

MOTHER: there's even a roof above the statue

FATHER: there's a huge stone photographic reproduction of his wife, thousands and thousands

MOTHER: towering over my little girl

FATHER: fifteen thousand, twenty thousand

MOTHER: this old Greek bitch's grave is

FATHER: twenty-five thousand pounds at least

MOTHER: towering over my little girl's

FATHER: Our precious baby

MOTHER: who slipped away from us

FATHER: out little girl lying there in the ground with a husband that never even visits,

MOTHER: dirty

FATHER: too busy selling, too busy with his job, his precious job to notice

MOTHER: Greek

FATHER: to notice our little angel slipping away from him.

MOTHER: cunt.

Pause. They exchange a look.

FATHER: The hardest part was getting the sledgehammer over the wall.

MOTHER: I passed it to him.

FATHER: I mean pitch black, I nearly broke my foot.

MOTHER: I passed it to him over the wall.

FATHER: And I took it and – do you know something – I knew the way.

MOTHER: of course he knew the way

FATHER: Pitch black and I knew the way.

MOTHER: four times a week, more on birthdays and Christmas, of course he knew the way

FATHER: And I'm standing there in front of Mrs Keriakous' monument

MOTHER: nineteen months since our baby

FATHER: and I felt

power.

I did.

I felt…power. I felt power over money. I felt righteous. I felt that this was an act of goodness, of the triumph of the little man. Or something.

And

I lifted the sledgehammer and cracked it down on the Virgin Mary's skull and I felt fantastic. I swung it into the columns and I felt God-like as they cracked, as they exploded into white dust, I felt like I had molten iron running through my veins when the roof caved in and I laughed when the stone photographic representation cracked into three pieces and fell to the floor.

I felt like my girl was…

Being brought back.

I felt like my Jess was being brought back into life.

Beat.

MOTHER: He sprayed 'greaseball' on the ruins

FATHER: make it look like vandalism

MOTHER: make it look random

FATHER: pissed all over it

MOTHER: Bit much.

FATHER: took a shit on her broken face

MOTHER: I didn't like that

FATHER: Stupid fucking Greek bitch, my daughter, my
daughter

MOTHER: We did what we had to do.

FATHER: And we made love that night.

MOTHER: Well you don't have to say that.

FATHER: Sorry. We did though.

Pause.

He was…

broken.

He was shattered into pieces.

MOTHER: Well, he shouldn't have

FATHER: Mr Keriakous, he cried and cried.

MOTHER: it shouldn't be allowed

FATHER: It was like she had died all over again.

MOTHER: such big monuments, grotesque

FATHER: I felt so

MOTHER: Weak.

FATHER: bad

MOTHER: you're just being weak

FATHER: Pouring out of him, this

MOTHER: vulgarity

FATHER: grief

MOTHER: Your daughter, for Christ's sake

FATHER: Pouring out of this little man

MOTHER: Your effing daughter!

FATHER: and I just

MOTHER: 'we're not rich' you said

FATHER: felt like I'd taken that sledgehammer to his wife

MOTHER: 'she does have a husband' you said

FATHER: I felt like I'd smashed his wife's body into pulp in front of his eyes

MOTHER: 'she'll never make it if we keep bailing her out'

FATHER: I've never seen a person so

MOTHER: 'she'll never learn'

FATHER: broken

MOTHER: 'we had to learn' like you've ever learnt anything

FATHER: so shattered

MOTHER: like you've ever learnt to do anything apart from lose things.

Beat. He turns to her.

FATHER: I still love you.

Pause.

MOTHER: He's having it rebuilt.

FATHER: Just the same.

MOTHER: Money to burn.

FATHER: Exactly the same.

MOTHER: Well, we'll see what happens.

Won't we.

Beat.

Won't we.

Beat.

I said we'll see, won't we.

No answer.

THREE

VAL, DAVID and PAUL in an office. They are all laughing.

VAL: ...go on, tell him

DAVID: No

VAL: Tell Paul about your award

DAVID: it's nothing, it's

VAL: It's not nothing

DAVID: No, come on

VAL: He's so modest, you're so modest

DAVID: it's no big deal, I just got this award for

VAL: it's no big deal, listen to this

DAVID: I just got this award for a short story that I wrote.

VAL: See? See?

DAVID: It was nothing, it was local, a local

VAL: Don't be falsely modest, David, it's repulsive.

DAVID: It was an award

VAL: Paul's never won an award, have you Paul, I've never won an award, I've never won anything

DAVID: a local paper, I mean

VAL: and what was it called

DAVID: (*Laughing.*) Now, don't, because

VAL: (*Laughing.*) you tell him

DAVID: because that's not fair

VAL: tell him, tell him

DAVID: you're gonna kick me out

VAL: I will kick you out if you don't bloody well tell him!

DAVID: Okay, look; it was called:

The Photosynthesist.

They laugh. PAUL wants to laugh but he doesn't get the joke.

VAL: Tell him what I thought photosynthesis was.

DAVID: She thought photosynthesis was

stealing photographs.

They laugh harder. Beat. PAUL joins in.

VAL: Thick or what?

DAVID: It sounds like it could be though, doesn't it

VAL: what a cunt

DAVID: it does sound a little

VAL: they didn't let me live that one down

DAVID: well…

VAL: It's something boring that happens with plants, Paul.

DAVID: funny.

VAL: perhaps, yeah. You had to be there.

Pause.

Look, I can give you a job, David.

DAVID: Can you?

VAL: Yes.

Beat.

DAVID: Good. Excellent.

VAL: If that's what you want?

DAVID: Yeah. It is.

VAL: Is that really what you want? A job here?

DAVID: Only if you have one.

VAL: In this? Commerce?

DAVID: Only if you have one, Val, I'm not asking you to make one for me.

VAL: I don't have one. I'd have to make one for you.

DAVID: Right.

VAL: David?

Beat.

DAVID: Could you make one for me?

VAL: Of course I can. I could, couldn't I Paul?

PAUL: Yes, you could. You definitely could.

VAL: I don't have one, but I could make one for you.

Pause.

DAVID: Okay then. Look, Val, could you make one for me?

VAL: Is this you?

DAVID: I think it could be.

VAL: And how are you going to feel working for me?

DAVID: Fine.

VAL: Fine?

DAVID: Yes, fine.

Pause.

VAL: You were always very proud.

DAVID: Val, if you're gonna be my boss you're –

VAL: You say that now, but how will you feel in six months' time?

DAVID: Fine.

VAL: You keep saying fine.

DAVID: Because it's fine.

VAL: And what does Jess feel? About you working for me?

DAVID: Fine.

VAL: You keep saying fine.

DAVID: Because it is fine.

VAL: I'm just asking you.

DAVID: Sorry, I didn't mean it like –

VAL: You see, I haven't even employed you and already –

DAVID: No, I didn't mean it like…you got the wrong end of the –

VAL: Did I? What did I get the wrong end of?

Pause.

DAVID: If you employ me I will be aware of where the boundaries are because –

VAL: Because I'll sack you if you're not, just like any other employee, but that's not what I'm worried about, what I'm worried about is you.

DAVID: I'm fine. I will be fine. I'm not as proud as you think I –

Pause.

It's easy to swan around saying this or that's shit when you're younger –

VAL: Do you think this is shit?

DAVID: No…

VAL: Do you think sales is shit?

DAVID: No, I –

VAL: Do you think telecommunications is beneath you?

DAVID: Val, I don't

VAL: soiling your hands –

DAVID: I don't think that, Val.

VAL: I'm just asking. It's fine, David I'm just asking a question, we're having a chat here and I'm just asking a question.

DAVID: I do not think sales is –

VAL: And this is an interview situation so you shouldn't really say shit, but never mind.

DAVID: I don't want you to do me any favours, Val, that's not what I'm here for.

VAL: I would be doing you a favour.

Pause.

DAVID: I love teaching, but –

VAL: Well, teaching.

PAUL: We'd all love to teach.

VAL: Five star life on a two star salary.

PAUL: Fucking disaster.

DAVID: The problem is I don't have a background in sales, so –

VAL: David, that is not a problem.

DAVID: No?

PAUL: Not at all.

VAL: Do you see anyone from college?

DAVID: No. Yes, I see Claire sometimes.

VAL: How is she? She hated me.

DAVID: No she didn't.

VAL: Well, she didn't like me.

DAVID: You used to say that about everyone.

VAL: That's because none of them liked me.

DAVID: They did, they–

VAL: They didn't, David. When we split up they were all of a sudden your friends, not mine.

DAVID: That's just the way –

VAL: David, for Christ's sake, what makes you think I care about it now? They didn't like me, I know they didn't, I was 'uncool'. It's years later. Who gives a shit?

Pause.

DAVID: Well, I suppose, maybe…

VAL: See?

DAVID: Yes.

VAL: I would be doing you a favour.

DAVID: That's what I'm here for; I'm here to ask you for a favour.

VAL: I'm not saying that to rub it in, I'm just saying that because I'm thinking about your pride.

DAVID: I'm not proud anymore.

VAL: Did you dump me because I was a Christian?

Beat.

DAVID: Look, the moment I said that about me not being able to reconcile myself to your beliefs I instantly regretted –

VAL: I think we can make a job for you. We can can't we, Paul?

PAUL: We can.

DAVID: Can you?

PAUL: Oh, yeah.

VAL: So why did you always tell me that they liked me?

DAVID: What do you mean?

VAL: What do you think I mean?

DAVID: They didn't hate you –

VAL: They didn't like me though did they.

DAVID: They didn't not like you, they just didn't actually like you.

VAL: So why did you always say that they liked me? You insisted that they liked me, I used to say to you they don't like me, it's you they like, they don't like me at all, and you'd say no, no, they like you, they really do.

DAVID: I suppose I was just… I didn't want you to feel…bad.

VAL: I did feel bad.

Pause.

David? I did feel bad.

DAVID: I didn't want you to.

VAL: So you lied. You did, you lied.

DAVID: Yes, but only to make you feel –

VAL: You basically said that I was wrong that I was imagining it all and that I was making it up and was just paranoid, but I knew I wasn't.

DAVID: I'm sorry.

VAL: But the thing is I'm not that person anymore. I've learnt a lot and I've learnt that although they all liked to take the piss out of my beliefs

DAVID: No-one took the piss –

VAL: They all believed in something just as powerfully but they didn't know that they did, and they pretended it was other things they believed in, do you follow me?

DAVID: I'm not sure if I –

VAL: Paul used to be a socialist

PAUL: Still vote Labour.

VAL: I don't believe in God anymore.

DAVID: No?

VAL: No I don't. Do I Paul.

PAUL: You definitely don't.

VAL: What do I believe in now, Paul?

PAUL: Cash.

VAL: Money. I believe in money.

David.

That's my thing now.

David.

And in the same way that a plant takes oxygen and nutrients and uses the process of photosynthesis to turn sunlight into energy, I take customers and employees and use the process of hard fucking work to produce cash.

I am a photosynthesist of cash.

Beat.

Paul?

PAUL hands her an application form. She hands it to DAVID.

You have to fill this in now, David.

DAVID: Okay.

VAL: I already know what you can do and what qualifications you've got but you have to fill it in just because –

DAVID: Because I have to fill it in.

VAL: Because you have to fill it in, of course. So, we can start you in the stockroom and –

DAVID: In the stockroom?

VAL: Yes.

Pause.

Did you expect sales straightaway?

DAVID: Well. I… I suppose I…

VAL: But you don't have a background in sales.

DAVID: That's why I came to you. Look, I mean I'm not expecting you to do me any favours –

VAL: I am doing you a favour.

DAVID: Yes, sorry. But I thought…

Pause.

I mean I thought I might get something…

VAL: You didn't think here?

PAUL: Here?

VAL: In management?

DAVID: I don't know what I thought, I thought (*Noticing something on the form.*) Jesus, I can't live on that.

VAL: It's low.

DAVID: Val, I can't –

VAL: It's a starting salary.

PAUL: Once you get into sales. I drive an Audi.

DAVID: That's less than I'm getting –

VAL: It's a starting salary, but once you get into sales –

DAVID: I need money now.

VAL: There's a grading system, we have to start you at grade two.

DAVID: What grade did you start at?

VAL: Grade five. But I've got a degree in business studies.

DAVID: I've got a degree.

VAL: English Literature. You've got a degree in English Literature, David. It's the only way, isn't it Paul?

PAUL: It is.

DAVID: Where did you start?

PAUL: Grade five.

VAL: But that's different.

DAVID: Val, I fucking need money.

Beat.

VAL: Paul, could you give us as minute.

PAUL gets up and goes out. DAVID goes to apologise but she silences him with a gesture. Beat.

Have you ever sucked a man's cock?

DAVID: What?

VAL: That's a way of making money.

DAVID: Val –

VAL: You or Jess could suck men's cocks, take pictures of it and sell them on the internet.

He sort of laughs. She doesn't. Beat.

I know someone who does it. Serious. He makes quite big chunks of cash that way.

DAVID: No, I'm not going to suck men's cocks.

VAL: I know you're not. I know you're not, David. I'm just trying to tell you that, yes, there are quick ways you can make money, but in general you have to do it the hard way. In fact it's all the hard way. If it wasn't you wouldn't get money for it. Did you ever get that mole checked out?

DAVID: What?

VAL: I was always nagging at you to get it checked out. Did you ever get it checked out?

DAVID: No. No I –

VAL: Can I see it?

Beat.

DAVID: What?

VAL: Can I see it?

Beat. He roles up his sleeve. She gets up, comes over and inspects the mole on his forearm. She looks at him. She reaches out and touches it with her finger. Pushes it. Beat. Licks it. Beat. Goes back to her seat. He rolls his sleeve back down.

Keep your head down, get on with stuff. I'll look after you. Really.

FOUR

1: You want to feel that not every working day is like wading through blood.

2: You want to feel there is more to life than just getting through it with the least possible amount of discomfort

1: there's that thing about live to work and work to live and I can't remember which one is the right one, but perhaps – despite what the world seems to tell us, despite the general feeling in, let's face it, what has become an almost terminally cynical world

3: perhaps it's possible to care about what you do

1: perhaps it's possible to believe in what you do

3: perhaps it's possible to believe in something, for Christ's sake

1: I mean how many hours are you spending at work? a third of your life, a quarter?

2: You want to do something that you feel, okay, and you're not some kind of, but…proud of.

1: So you try.

3: you work, you work hard to do better

2: yes

3: Because it's not wrong

2: yes, yes

1: to believe.

4: yes

1: it's not wrong to want to believe in something.

JESS: When I was a child I saw this programme on aliens and I suddenly realised with absolute clarity that I was an alien, I realised that my mother had been impregnated with alien spores and that was why when all the other kids were laughing at cartoons or something, a moose or a cat I think it was, getting killed, I would be horrified and wonder why they were laughing at such terrible things and I spent a good four years terrified that the CIA were going to take me away for some sort of bio-military experimentation.

4: You work for a credit card company

5: let's say

4: you are in charge of policy

5: for example

4: okay, you'd rather be a movie star or a footballer or a super model or an aid worker in the Sudan, but you aren't and you're happy, with, you've done well to get this far, you do a job, you do it well, you get on with it

5: you're a good person

4: not perfect

2: no-one's perfect

4: you hate it when your friends do well

5: but you feel terrible for feeling like that

4: an ordinary fucking human fucking being

3: so let's not judge

4: You have ideas, for Christ's sake, you think, you have an imagination

3: you want to do well for your family

2: there are children

5: one of each

3: a girl of three and her eighteen-month-old brother

4: a three-year-old girl who looks just like your partner and it's funny because she's even beginning to act a little bit like her, and that is funny to see this tiny version of someone you know so well growing

5:   you argue about money

2:   but you also argue about telly and child-care

3:   And one day you have this idea

4:   Yes.

You have this idea.

JESS: I sometimes fantasise about when I become an alcoholic, hiding bottles, unable to do anything without a drink and people talking about me and saying 'it's such a shame, she's so talented' and being admitted to a treatment centre where I fight against them with all my might but eventually succumb to the inevitable logic of the twelve-step programme before finally telling my story of triumph over degradation, but to be honest if I drink more than one bottle of wine I get sick.

2:   You happen to notice that a large amount of the people you turn down for credit get their credit from other sources

1:   not so reputable sources

3:   but these days you can always get credit

2:   and they pay incredibly high rates of interest

1:   sometimes the equivalent of an annual interest of ninety-five percent, one hundred percent

2:   you've heard of as high as a hundred and sixty percent

4:   and you wonder about offering

2:   not the package they've applied for

1:   no

3:   and sorry if this is boring, but it's actually quite exciting

2: but a different credit package for people whose credit is too bad for the one that they've applied for

3: See? See?

2: and of course because their credit is bad they pay more money

3: which makes sense

1: less, actually, than they would be paying to the less reputable sources, so you're sort of doing them a favour

4: business, this is how business

2: and you look at the amount to be made on the interest repayments

1: and you look at the amount to be lost on the people who default

5: and you take the second sum away from the first sum and you realise that the difference is a sizable chunk of cash

3: a very sizable chunk of profit for your company and its shareholders

4: and your job is to make more profit for your company and its shareholders, that's what having shareholders is all about, that is the point of

2: and you realise that this is one of those ideas. You know? One of those ideas that come along, one of those great ideas. And you somehow feel that this great idea – and this may be silly – that this great idea has been given to you from a higher source

3: that's silly

2: that is silly, and you know that's silly, and you don't believe that, but that's how it feels

3: and you know that this is your chance, the world is holding out its hand, there is some kind of alignment going on, a portal or something, and it'll only last for seconds, alright, maybe not, but it feels that way, it feels…

2: and you know that someone else is bound to have this idea, any day now, ideas like this, they don't hang around long

5: and the question you have to ask is 'Are you the person who sat on the sidelines?'

1: 'Are you the person who watched?'

2: The question you have to ask is simple: 'What kind of person are you?'

JESS: Last week I was standing in front of this window staring at this bag that I couldn't afford, and – it was a really nice bag, it was – and I felt like, I felt like I couldn't move, I couldn't leave because of the bag, I mean physically I was rooted to the spot and all the hair was standing up on the back of my neck and I felt terrible because I was getting so emotional about a fucking bag and meanwhile there's still no sign of a two-state solution in the Middle East and it suddenly dawned on me that the bag was designed, not to hold things, but to hold me and it was like hearing for the first time and I felt so elated at this discovery that I immediately went in and bought it because it no longer held power over me, and I felt brilliant for the rest of the day. But when I thought about it again that evening it just seemed…

stupid.

She laughs.

I cried.

1: It. Works. Beautifully.

4: Increased turnover of thirty, thirty-five million in the first year alone, it's attractive

3: people are attracted to it

5:   and you made it, it's something you made

1:   and you're rewarded

2:   and you're promoted

4:   pay upgrades, yes, and bonuses

1:   and the respect of people around you and you notice that
     when you are introduced to people they already know
     who you are and sometimes they raise an eyebrow and say
     'Oh', in recognition before shaking your hand

4:   which is nice

5:   that is nice

2:   and maybe you start thinking about a new child

3:   maybe?

2:   Things are good.

1:   Things are really good.

JESS: I'm thinking about becoming a Buddhist because I am
     attracted to its philosophies of acceptance, of being, of
     being in the moment, of the idea of being on a journey and
     its attraction to the universal but I can't decide if it's the
     right thing to do because on the one hand David Lynch is a
     Buddhist but on the other so is Richard Gere.

     I've also thought about becoming an evangelist Christian,
     a tramp, some form of terrorist, a communist and a lap
     dancer, actually, actually, actually anything

     that

     isn't

     me. I suppose.

1:   But…

     your mind might find itself wandering back to those figures

4:   yes

2: to the second sum

5: the defaulters

3: things are still good

2: oh yes, things are still good, but your mind might find itself wandering back to the people in that second sum, and you might, though you try not to think about it, you might find yourself thinking of some of those figures as

4: people

2: because they are, really

4: you're not responsible,

2: No, of course

3: we're all adults for Christ's

2: but

4: you're not responsible, but

2: you might think about these people

3: and their hardship, and that's a stupid word, yes, like something out of the nineteenth century, yes, but it keeps coming back into your head

2: hardship, it's stupid but hardship

1: and you might find yourself thinking that what one person does to another is a thing. Like a real thing. And that systems and numbers and the way we do those things are in some way not real, even though everything we have ever learnt has taught us to believe that they are real, you might now come to believe that in actual fact they aren't, and the only thing that is real is the thing that you have done to another human being. And strangely you begin to feel alone. Separate. And you might begin to think – and this is silly – but you might begin to think of something you saw on a documentary, a card written in German that was part of a filing system – and this is really not the same

247

at all, it's ridiculous – but you might think of the person who put those terrible figures on that card, and that they must've thought of them as figures and figures only and you might wonder how they managed to live with, and though this is silly and though this is ridiculous and though you know you're being stupid and that this really is not the same at all you know that in some way it might be, in the mechanics of how you actually do something, and you can't get the image of the fucking card out of your fucking head.

Pause.

5: And you might think of someone

4: a woman

5: a woman

1: at odd moments

2: when you're out with friends, giving a presentation, making love to your partner

3: the image of someone

4: a woman

5: overwhelmed

1: a woman

2: overwhelmed

3: and no, it's not just the fault of, I mean there are contributing factors

2: maybe this woman never felt

4: at one with

3: but I mean who fucking

5: the world

3: who fucking does

1:   but you begin to see this woman again and again, but in greater clarity, like you know her

3:   like you are her, or something

2:   not are her, but are part of her, I don't know, I mean are we a part of each other? aren't we part of…

1:   and you feel her becoming overwhelmed with…life and maybe just trying to fucking well fit in, I mean isn't that what we're all, isn't that what you are trying, aren't we just trying to do what we think someone like us is supposed to be doing?

4:   and you might suddenly feel her panic

5:   her confusion

1:   you might suddenly feel her panic and confusion overwhelming

JESS: I'm staring at these forks, just standing there in this shop staring at these forks in my hands and praying for a sign like one set of forks, the squared-off three-prong brushed steel ones for example, are going to suddenly get heavier as a sign that I should put back the curved, silver, more weighty, more traditional Terence Malone forks, but then I thought would the forks getting heavier be a sign that I should put them back or that I should keep them and a sweat broke out on my forehead, I felt prickles in my armpits and suddenly I felt the cold that sat around my heart like a blanket of oil creep out and begin to expand into the rest of my body and I thought 'Here we go. This is it. Here we fucking go' and I don't remember the rest.

Beat.

1:   And you might see her on a ward.

3:   Gone crazy in a shop, of all things

1:   crying, screaming

2:   panicking, actually, real terror

4: and she's taken to a ward

2: Sectioned.

4: Only a weekend, but…

1: just a weekend, you might see her in there for just a weekend, but

2: When her husband visits, he's

5: shocked

4: he's shocked

1: not so much at her, she looks, I mean she's unhappy

3: embarrassed, if anything

1: but she's not too

4: but the people around her are, I mean he didn't expect

5: dribbling

3: and rocking

2: he didn't expect

5: a ward

4: he should've done because they said she was on a ward but he didn't expect

3: he's frustrated

1: he counts thirteen people that have seen his wife in that one weekend, she's telling the same stuff thirteen different times

Beat.

And maybe, while you're going about your daily business, getting a coffee

2: playing hide and seek with your little girl and letting her win

1: you're doing these things but this story is still running through your brain

2: and you imagine this man, you imagine him

5: this teacher

4: you imagine him…

1: He sits there in their living room.

3: He spreads out everything on the floor.

2: He has a pad and a pen and a calculator that he nicked from work, statements, bills, invoices even.

3: that weekend, that very night, after having to leave his wife in that place, and he's

2: He's shocked

1: again he's shocked because he understands that all the numbers and figures and pounds and red letters add up to a void

2: a void in her that he should be filling

5: shouldn't he?

1: And then he finds your great idea.

2: And he finds your beautiful idea.

4: and he cries.

3: He cries deep from within his insides.

1: And he wonders how it ever got to this.

Pause.

5: He resolves to get through it.

JESS: I'm feeling much better

5: He's going to get both of them through it.

JESS: I'm feeling great actually

5: He's gonna get a new job

JESS: Back in the real world

5: He thinks he knows where he can get a job that pays, real money

JESS: I'm not taking time off

5: He's gonna get a job that pays, get her back home, tell her how much he loves her and start putting things right

2: He loves her

5: and she loves him.

2: but you…

5: you…

Beat.

1: You might no longer want another child.

2: You might not be able to look your partner in the face.

1: You might find that food now tastes the same.

3: like plastic

1: You might find that eating food is like putting plastic into your mouth.

4: You might find that you are increasingly prone to dark moods

2: and you might wonder how to get rid of this feeling

4: and you might drink

3: and you might sleep with strangers

2: and you might buy stuff and buy stuff and buy stuff

1: and you might find that nothing, nothing, works

2: and you may have this terrible fear that

4: and you might have this terrible fear

1: and you may have this terrible fear that every day, working or otherwise will actually be like wading through blood.

FIVE

DEBBIE and DUNCAN in a shitty pub, DUNCAN leaving, slightly drunk.

DUNCAN: (*Pointing at the card on the table.*) You've got my card?

DEBBIE: Yes.

DUNCAN: You know where to get me?

DEBBIE: Yes.

DUNCAN: S'up to you.

DEBBIE: Right.

DUNCAN: There's lots of ways we can take this. Lots of possibilities. Take this any way you want.

DEBBIE: Right.

DUNCAN: I'm not a fruit bat. You got my card.

DEBBIE: Yes, thanks.

DUNCAN: You can see, can't you.

DEBBIE: Oh yeah.

DUNCAN: Not taking the piss.

DEBBIE: No.

DUNCAN: Not a cunt.

DEBBIE: No.

DUNCAN: Long as you don't treat me like a cunt, that's all I ask of anyone. You're waiting for someone. I'll go. Forgive me. But there's lots of ways we can take this.

DEBBIE: Right.

DUNCAN: Have you given any thought to where you want to take this?

DEBBIE: No, I –

DUNCAN sits back down.

DUNCAN: Don't worry about that yet. That's my job. That's what I get my percentage for. Swallowing vomit, this place. Animals. Fucking animals. Have you given it any thought?

DEBBIE: No.

DUNCAN: You don't need to. This is filth. This is real dirt. You don't need to be in real dirt. Acting. Modelling. Singing. There's all sorts of ways.

DEBBIE: What, really?

DUNCAN: All sorts of ways. Have you ever felt that you were meant for something better?

DEBBIE: No.

DUNCAN: They should napalm this lot. Makes me sick. Get Bin Laden round here. You just need to know the options. I walk out there, I got Kurds shitting on my doorstep. You're better than that. Have you thought much about TV?

DEBBIE: No.

DUNCAN: No. Course you have. Everyone's thought about TV. Don't call me a cunt. Anyways. You're waiting for someone. I'll wade off through this crowd of diarrhoea. The great British public. Cunts. Have you thought of them shows?

DEBBIE: Which shows?

DUNCAN: Saturday night, millions of viewers. Think. Think, think, think. But let me do the thinking. You see, there you display your naivety, Debbie, but if you weren't naive people like me wouldn't exist.

DEBBIE: No.

DUNCAN: (*Getting up.*) Out of the blue, I'm not some sort of cunt, yes, I'm lonely, boo fucking hoo, but this isn't that, this isn't about that. My business this is the way it works; you see, you strike, do you understand, Debbie?

DEBBIE: Yeah.

DUNCAN: Do you understand?

DEBBIE: Yes.

DUNCAN: Do you understand, Debbie?

DEBBIE: I think so.

Beat. DUNCAN sits down again.

DUNCAN: I wanna show you something.

DEBBIE: Okay.

DUNCAN: Because I think we've made a bond.

DEBBIE: Thank you.

DUNCAN: You're waiting, I know, one minute, I wanna show you something.

He pulls out a Polaroid-type photo out of his pocket. They look at it for a long time.

It's a man with a cock in his mouth.

DEBBIE: I know.

DUNCAN: You see?

DEBBIE: Yeah, I don't really think –

DUNCAN: (*Putting it away.*) No, of course.

DEBBIE: I don't –

DUNCAN: Absolutely.

DEBBIE: It's just –

DUNCAN: It's just, it's just, I'm putting it away, I'm putting it right fucking away, but you understand it's my job to cover all bases.

DEBBIE: I see.

DUNCAN: Lots of fucking ways, Debbie, lots of fucking ways this can be taken.

Beat.

Six hundred quid. Plus expenses.

But forget that.

Look at that barman.

DEBBIE: Which –

DUNCAN: Yeah. I see people like him I want to cry. What the fuck's the point? Do you know why? Because I've been there. It's about sacrifice. The things I've had to sacrifice. My wife won't touch me. I started off with pets.

DEBBIE: Pets?

DUNCAN: Pets. Pet models. Adverts. What? Please, you think when they want to sell dog-shit gravel they just pop down Battersea? Nothing works like that. I got one client, his dog's got his own bedroom. Bought it a telly. Sandwiches and Müller Fruit Corners for lunch. What? You think that's excessive? You got a dog?

DEBBIE: No.

DUNCAN: Well if you did have its lifestyle would cost you more than the average yearly earnings of the majority of the population of Eritrea. It's a sick world. I don't blame her. I wouldn't touch me if I didn't have to. We had a boy once. Leukaemia.

DEBBIE: No.

DUNCAN: Yeah.

DEBBIE: That's awful.

DUNCAN: Yeah. Tore her into shreds. Aged twenty years in a weekend. Don't wash, doesn't smile, breath like disease.

DEBBIE: Jesus.

DUNCAN: Ah well, you know what they say: life's a cunt and then you get old as well. This is filth. This is really filth. There's a lot of ways we can take this, Debbie. You've got my card.

DEBBIE: Yes.

DUNCAN: You know where I am.

DEBBIE: Yes.

DUNCAN: (*Getting up.*) I'm off then.

DEBBIE: Well thank you.

DUNCAN: (*Picking up a beer mat.*) Can I take this?

DEBBIE: Well…

DUNCAN: (*Picking up one of her dog ends.*) And this?

DEBBIE: Er, yeah, I –

DUNCAN: I'm not gonna lie it's so I can be near you. You see what I am? Please don't laugh at me.

DEBBIE: I'm not, I'm not laughing.

DUNCAN: You should laugh, you should laugh at the idea of this dirty old man crying himself to sleep at night holding your fucking beer mat, it's sad, it's disgusting, I'm disgusting

DEBBIE: You're not disgusting.

Beat. Sits back down.

DUNCAN: What's the one thing you love about modern life most?

DEBBIE: Erm…

DUNCAN: No erm.

DEBBIE: I suppose…

DUNCAN: Yes?

DEBBIE: I dunno.

DUNCAN: Think.

DEBBIE: Well, maybe, the travel; you can go on holidays –

DUNCAN: No, not the travel.

DEBBIE: No?

DUNCAN: No, something else.

DEBBIE: The telly's quite –

DUNCAN: Something else.

DEBBIE: I…

DUNCAN: Less physical.

DEBBIE: I like, I think there's quite a lot of choice –

DUNCAN: It's not the choice, Debbie.

DEBBIE: What is it, then?

DUNCAN: I'm asking you, I'm asking you what you love most.

DEBBIE: Right. I think, oh right, I think it's the
communication, so many ways, now, we can –

DUNCAN: No.

DEBBIE: Is it bars and pubs? like better, some better, going out
some are better, than they used to

You know.

Beat.

DUNCAN: No, it's not that.

Belief.

It's belief.

The absolute conviction that all this is right.

DEBBIE: Right.

DUNCAN: Only we don't really, do we, Debs. That's the great
secret. Not in our heart of hearts.

Pause.

Tell me something about you.

DEBBIE: What do you mean?

DUNCAN: The real Debbie. 'Who is the real Debbie?'

DEBBIE: I'm just me.

DUNCAN: Something you've never told anyone else…

DEBBIE: I don't think…

DUNCAN: Please. Let me in, Debbie. Touch me.

Pause. She thinks.

DEBBIE: I put wall-paper paste in the coffee machine at work.

Beat.

You know the powder, you buy the powder in, while no-
one was looking I put it into the machine and stirred it all
in and left it and it clogged up the machine and they all
stood around it staring at it, hurt, like it was a dead puppy.

Beat.

When you print orders at work, they come out face up
with the address on, on, on the front and you never see
the backs until they, you know, come back from the clients
completed, the order form is on the back, you see, so
you never see the, until, so I stayed late one night and I
photocopied the word 'cock' on the back of all the order
forms, with a big picture of a cock and balls that I drew
in magic marker, and then I put them back in the printer,
and the next day they sent out thousands and they got
hundreds of complaints and lost their two biggest clients.

I keep falling asleep in meetings and no-one's noticed yet. They think I'm concentrating.

Last week I caught a mouse in my flat, I have mice, which is something I don't really, I don't really like that, I have mice and I caught this one on glue paper, you know, the glue traps, I've tried everything else and that's the only thing that works and the worst thing is that when you catch them they're still alive so you have to, you know, despatch them, so I put a cloth over it and I hit it on the head with a cup, a mug, but it took quite a few, you know, hits and it was screaming and I felt sick and I was crying and everything and then I peeled it off the paper, you have to be very careful because the body's quite delicate, and then I took a scalpel that I have for handicrafts and I slit its little belly open and I tugged out all its insides and I stuck them and the body onto this Christmas card, so that it was splayed open with the guts out into this Christmas tree design, and I sent it to my boss with writing cut out from a newspaper saying 'Thanks for all the hard work and good luck in the new job cunt-face'. They called the police.

Beat.

I wanted to be a newsreader when I was a little girl.

Pause. She picks up the card. He stares at her.

DUNCAN: (*Pointing at the ashtray.*) That your chewing gum?

DEBBIE: Yeah

DUNCAN: Can I take it?

Beat.

DEBBIE: Well…

DUNCAN: Am I making you sick?

DEBBIE: It just seems a bit

DUNCAN: Weird?

DEBBIE: Weird, yes.

DUNCAN: I understand.

I want to take it and put it in my mouth and chew on it because I think that by chewing on something that someone like you has chewed on something of you will become some part of me, like I might become infected by your goodness.

DEBBIE: Well…

Beat.

She nods. He takes the chewing gum from the ashtray, puts it in his mouth and starts chewing on it.

DUNCAN: You really do all that? With the mouse and that?

She doesn't answer.

Not like this once you're a client. I'm a professional.

You're very easy to talk to.

DEBBIE: Am I?

DUNCAN: One of your strengths. Like a priest. We should remember that. Capitalise on that. Chat shows, maybe.

DEBBIE: Right.

DUNCAN: He was a teacher.

Beat.

The man…

Makes blowjob sign.

DEBBIE: Right.

DUNCAN: Or something. Nice fella. Married. In debt. You know the sort. We're all dealing with something, Debs, we're all trying to fill some gap. Make a decision, Debbie. Stop fucking around.

DEBBIE: Well –

DUNCAN: So many ways we can take this. I think a lot about the future. I used to like thinking about dinosaurs when I was at school but now it's just the future.

I'd like an item of your clothing?

Please.

DEBBIE: What?

DUNCAN: Please. Please, Debbie, just to let me know that you're real.

DEBBIE: My clothing?

DUNCAN: Yes. That's what I'd like. That's what I'm asking for.

DEBBIE: It just seems…

DUNCAN: Sign of good faith.

Pause.

Debbie?

DEBBIE: Like what?

DUNCAN: Handkerchief.

DEBBIE: Handkerchief, I haven't got a –

DUNCAN: What else?

Sock?

DEBBIE: I can't walk around in one sock.

DUNCAN: S'that a jumper?

DEBBIE: That's quite expensive.

DUNCAN: I just want something

DEBBIE: It cost, it's quite an –

DUNCAN: Your knickers.

DEBBIE: What?

DUNCAN: Please. I want to be dead.

Pause. She takes her knickers off and gives them to him. He puts them away. He gets up.

I was young once. Glad it's over. It was like love.

SIX

(*JESS sits in a hospital waiting room. She is deep in thought. She stays like that for a while. There is blood on her sleeves. DAVID enters.*)

DAVID: Fucking hell

JESS: I know

DAVID: Are you alright?

JESS: Yeah

DAVID: really?

JESS: yeah

DAVID: Are you?

JESS: Yeah, no I mean

DAVID: No?

JESS: No, I mean yeah, yeah, I am, I'm

DAVID: Are you?

JESS: Yes, please, stop

DAVID: are you sure, I mean have they fucking seen you or what?

JESS: Look there's nothing wrong with me, don't get all

DAVID: I mean is there anyone here?

JESS: clingy, because there's nothing

DAVID: doctors or, I mean fucking hell where is everybody?

JESS: busy, they're busy

DAVID: I mean have you spoken to anyone?

JESS: The police.

DAVID: Clingy?

JESS: Everything's

DAVID: I'm not clingy, I'm worried

JESS: fine

DAVID: Are you okay?

JESS: I am, I'm

DAVID: You've got blood on your sleeve, Jess.

She looks at her sleeve.

JESS: What?

Yeah, no, that's the man's

DAVID: The man's…blood?

JESS: Yes.

That's the man's blood.

He hugs her. They stay like that for a while.

DAVID: What happened?

JESS: He just stabbed

DAVID: Who, the man?

JESS: No, he stabbed the man.

DAVID: Who?

JESS: The other man

DAVID: Why did he stab him?

JESS: Because he bumped into him.

DAVID: He stabbed him because he bumped into him?

JESS: Yeah

DAVID: Because he bumped into him?

JESS: Yeah and

DAVID: Fuck

JESS: Yes, yeah, because he fucking

DAVID: What because he bumped into him?

JESS: Well, he was on the phone

DAVID: Who?

JESS: The man – no, sorry, the other man, the other man was on, he was on the phone, phoning he, and the man, he was running for a bus and the street was crowded so

DAVID: Where was this?

JESS: Oxford Street, he was running for a

DAVID: On Oxford Street?

JESS: Yes, he was, he was running for this

DAVID: On Oxford Street?

JESS: Yes, on, it was on Oxford Street, I said it was on Oxford Street

DAVID: Sorry

JESS: and he bumps into the other man and he knocks, right, and he knocks the phone out of his hands and it goes skittering

DAVID: The phone

JESS: yes, the phone, it goes skittering under this bus

DAVID: are you okay?

JESS: Yes I'm fine.

DAVID: under a bus?

JESS: yeah, yes, like in a joke or something

DAVID: Was it broken?

JESS: It was fucked

DAVID: Was it?

JESS: It was completely fucked

DAVID: You didn't say it was Oxford Street.

Beat.

When you phoned. When you phoned you didn't say it was Oxford Street

JESS: No, but I'm saying it now.

DAVID: Yeah, but you didn't then

JESS: Because a man had been stabbed in the chest, David.

DAVID: Right.

JESS: He was stabbed, he was stabbed in the chest.

DAVID: Okay, I'm just

JESS: What?

DAVID: No, nothing. Sorry, I'm just

JESS: He was dying, the man was

DAVID: Is that what they said, that he's dying?

JESS: No, they're not saying anything

DAVID: Why not?

JESS: Because they're trying to save his life.

DAVID: Why were you on Oxford Street?

Beat.

JESS: I was on my way to the fucking tube!

DAVID: I'm just asking, Jess.

JESS: He was stabbed!

DAVID: I know I'm just

JESS: Because of a phone

Because of a…thing.

Beat.

I think it was a Nokia.

DAVID: Was it?

JESS: Yeah, it was a, like Jane's.

DAVID: Jane's is a Nokia.

JESS: That's what I'm saying, and this man, the other man

DAVID: It's a nice phone

JESS: It's not that nice.

DAVID: Did he know he'd done it?

JESS: Who?

DAVID: The man.

JESS: No, he was just running for a bus

DAVID: right

JESS: I mean it was a bit rude and everything, but Jesus he didn't know he'd

DAVID: No

JESS: and this other man he was

DAVID: What did he look like?

JESS: The man?

DAVID: Yes.

JESS: Or the other man?

DAVID: The other man

JESS: Just like an ordinary man, just a man who's been to work and is making a call on his Nokia before getting on the bus

DAVID: Jesus Christ!

JESS: Late twenties, early thirties, maybe

DAVID: fucking animal

JESS: and he just pulls out this knife

DAVID: A big knife?

JESS: Yeah, yeah, a big fucking knife and he stabs him

DAVID: Jesus!

JESS: Just stabs him

DAVID: What's he doing with a fucking knife?

JESS: in the chest

DAVID: Fuck!

JESS: Yeah, yeah

DAVID: I mean do people walk around with fucking knives these days?

JESS: Just stabs him right in the chest, he just pushes it into him, right into his chest, he just pushes it into him. And the man steps back. Because the force, you know, because he's pushed so hard. He steps back a little, to keep his balance. And the other man pulls the knife out and blood just starts running down this man's chest like a leak.

DAVID: In the middle of Oxford Street?

JESS: It was like he was leaking, but quite a lot, you know. And then he just sort of, he sort of sat, just sort of gently sat on the pavement.

DAVID: And the other man?

JESS: He was gone.

And I just, I just, I was just, I just put my hands on him.

DAVID: On the man?

JESS: Yes.

DAVID: On his

JESS: Yes.

DAVID: wound?

JESS: Yes, I just

DAVID: You put your hands on his wound?

JESS: Yes, I just covered, I just, he was lying down, and, I just put my hands on the, like no-one else wanted, I mean I think they didn't want to get their clothes sticky or

DAVID: Cunts

JESS: no, no, because I think they just didn't think, because you don't

DAVID: no, but

JESS: and everyone's got such nice clothes these days

DAVID: Are you okay?

JESS: No, I'm fine.

> *Beat.*

> And an ambulance came. And I got in the ambulance with him. And I came here. With him.

> They took him in there

DAVID: In there?

JESS: Yes.

DAVID: You don't know how he is?

JESS: No.

DAVID: Right.

> *Long pause.*

> What tube?

JESS: What?

DAVID: What tube were you getting?

JESS: (*Beat.*) Leicester Square.

DAVID: Right.

That's not on Oxford Street.

JESS: No I was cutting through

DAVID: From?

JESS: What does it matter?

DAVID: I'm just asking.

JESS: Where I had my interview.

DAVID: Which was?

JESS: Poland Street.

DAVID: Right.

JESS: Where I had my interview.

DAVID: How did it go?

JESS: Pricks.

DAVID: So you didn't get the job?

JESS: No I got the job, but they're pricks.

DAVID: So you're not going to take it?

JESS: Of course I'm going to take it, I need a second job.

DAVID: And it's on Poland Street?

JESS: Yes.

Beat.

It was leaking out of him. It was like it was just leaking, just ebbing out of him and you'd see, you know, you could see him shutting down. You know? Like blood is what, I don't

know, we are, or something, just this liquid, like we're bags
of water walking around and one day someone pokes a
hole in the bag, and that's it, you know, end of story, you
start leaking and everything starts shutting down until you
close, just close down and then that's it.

I was worried that the blood would go somewhere it
shouldn't. Like I'd be blocking it and it would be jammed
and go back into his body and it might poison him because
it had gone into the wrong bit. I don't know if that happens
or if it's just a thought, I tried asking but they didn't know
what I was, so do you know if it does?

Beat.

If that happens?

DAVID: That's a detour.

JESS: What?

DAVID: Oxford Street. That's a detour.

JESS: No

DAVID: Yes, if you're on Poland Street and you're going to
Leicester Square then Oxford Street is a detour.

JESS: (*Beat.*) Is it?

DAVID: Yes. It is.

Beat.

JESS: Well, it's all near each other.

DAVID: But it's a detour

JESS: Who cares?

DAVID: Isn't it.

JESS: Yeah, but who

DAVID: Is it or isn't it?

JESS: Yeah, but it's all next to each other, so

DAVID: Is it or isn't it?

JESS: Yes, but

DAVID: Yes?

JESS: Yes, but

DAVID: Yes, then.

Yes, it's a detour.

Beat.

JESS: Fucking hell, David, a man's

DAVID: Right, it is then.

JESS: been stabbed, he's

DAVID: So you took a detour to Oxford Street.

JESS: lying in there

DAVID: Why?

JESS: What?

DAVID: Why?

Why? Why did you take a detour to Oxford Street?

Beat.

JESS: Why are you being like this?

DAVID: Because, Jess, because you had an interview on Poland Street which is, as far as I know, as far as I remember, which is south of Oxford Street, and you wanted to get to Leicester Square tube station, which as far as I can also remember, Jess, as far as I also know, if it hasn't fucking moved, Jess, is also south of Oxford Street. So what I'm wondering is what you were doing on Oxford Street? What I am trying to figure out, Jess, is for what reason my wife would take a large detour out of her way to go north to Oxford Street, which is without a doubt one of the most crowded, unpleasant, shitty streets in this city.

Pause.

JESS: Don't talk to me like that.

DAVID: Did you buy something?

No answer.

Did you?

No answer.

Did you go shopping?

No answer.

Is that what you did, you went shopping?

JESS: No.

DAVID: Jess? Is it?

JESS: Look –

DAVID: After everything we've been though? After you being in hospital?

JESS: Don't bring that up

DAVID: In a mental hospital, Jess, in a fucking, after all the shit and fucking, after me getting a crappy, shitty job, after all the things, things I've done that you don't even, the financial fucking, things you don't even

JESS: stop going on about money

DAVID: know about, we have to talk about money

JESS: a man's

DAVID: I want to talk about other things, I want to talk about the future and holidays and education, but instead we have to talk about money because

JESS: a man's been

DAVID: after the things I, after I –

JESS: he's been stabbed

DAVID: after I –

Beat.

Did you?

JESS: It's not like that!

Beat.

I bought some CDs.

I just bought some fucking CDs.

Okay? I didn't kill someone, I didn't fuck a stranger, I bought some CDs and then I watched a man get stabbed.

Beat.

I put my hands on him. I've still got his blood under my fingernails, I watched him shutting down because of a phone and I'm thinking is there anything else and is that it, is this all we are?

DAVID: Where are they?

Beat.

Can I see your CDs?

Beat. She shows him the CDs.

Good CDs. Nice

JESS: David –

Suddenly he gets up.

He goes to break the CDs. Doesn't.

He goes to walk out. Doesn't.

He goes to grab his hair. Doesn't.

He goes to throw the CDs. Doesn't.

He goes to say something. Doesn't.

He goes to almost hit her. Doesn't.

He goes to sit down. Doesn't.

He goes to put the CDs down. Doesn't.

He is in tears. Turns away as the DOCTOR enters. The DOCTOR stands there, awkward, not noticing that DAVID is crying. Pause.

JESS: Oh.

DOCTOR: Yes. Sorry.

JESS: Oh, no, it's okay.

DOCTOR: We did everything we could, the bleeding was just too

JESS: That's fine.

DOCTOR: severe, you did everything you could.

JESS: No, no, it's fine, honestly

DOCTOR: There's this sack that the, the heart sits in and unfortunately the bleeding leaked into this sack and once the sack

JESS: honestly, honestly

DOCTOR: ruptures

JESS: Yeah, no don't worry. I mean are you sure he's –

No, sorry, of course.

Silence.

DOCTOR: Are you going to be alright?

JESS: Yes.

DOCTOR: You've got someone here so...

You did everything you could.

JESS: Oh yeah, I know I'm fine, it's fine, I'm fine.

DOCTOR: There's a coffee machine at the end of the hall.

JESS: Great. Thank you. Thank you for that.

He goes. She sits.

After a while DAVID gets up.

DAVID: I'm going.

JESS: He's dead. The man's dead.

DAVID: I'm going home.

JESS: What about the man?

Pause.

David?

What about the man?

But DAVID goes.

SEVEN

JESS: I don't know if we're alone.

I don't think we want to be alone, do we? Do we want that? Is that what we want? And sometimes you think that the only reason we do anything at all, anything, is to reach out and touch

just touch, just to

feel

something

in our hand, I suppose and, or not in our hands in our hearts, or to reach with our souls and to find out that it's not all just dust and rocks and nuclear explosions in the hearts of stars with some accidentally organic matter moving around on one tiny minuscule planet. D'you know what I mean?

That connection?

Just to connect.

And you look around, don't you, and you think 'is this what it is? everyone else seems to think it's this, so that's what I'll do, I'll get a job and a house and the right shoes and I'll, you know, because this could be it' and I'm not saying it isn't and those things are great and I hate it when people are all critical and everything because we all wear

shoes

for Christ's sake, so, you know, but

sometimes I'm left

wondering

and I wonder if others are as

confused

and are also left wondering and maybe there is this entire planet of people wondering but pretending that we know exactly what we're doing and that we fit in perfectly and that we're not scared or confused or

lonely

or anything like that.

Beat.

And I might be saying this because I'm in love.

And

I might be looking for meaning because I'm in love

and what is that? alright, what

chemicals

or

electric pulses racing, yes, yes, but let me tell you – and I'm not arguing with all that – but let me tell you that what I feel is so

real

and tangible

and powerful and honest and torrential it screams through me sometimes and I want to vomit, I want to puke because I'm in love, isn't that fucked, I'm so in love I could puke.

Little laugh. Beat.

So I'm watching this programme last night and they're talking about this big problem in science, it's like this massive sort of, philosophical problem I suppose, and this problem is that the

universe

is just so fucking

unlikely

it's just so kind of

ridiculous, that it has turned out exactly this way that you've got to say

'hang on…

oh yeah, come on, pull the other one.'

And it's all to do with the values for gravity and the speed of light and electro-magnetic, you know, and these things, these values are set in the first few instants of the big bang, you know, you can't, we can't

go further

than that, our physics just doesn't work that far back, relativity breaks down at the moment of a singularity, blah, blah, blah, but once these

laws

come into

being, they stay, they stay as they are and that is that and they make up the universe, they, you know, you take gravity, for example, and you say right, in the beginning, just matter in clouds, but gravity means that matter attracts matter so matter clumps together forming stars and the gravity is pulling one way, squishing the atoms which causes nuclear explosions which is basically pushing the other way and this is basically, you know, how a star, that's how it works and you have these forces squishing the atoms over billions of years into heavier elements, new elements being formed in these stars which eventually explode and distribute those elements, which is us, which is everything, which is everything in the universe made up of stars, which I find fascinating in itself that we are all made of an ancient super-massive dead star, but that is another, I'm not going on about, that's a sidetrack, but the thing is

that gravity

just happens to be set

at the perfect level for this to happen.

Just happens to be that. So say gravity is like one hundred in ten thousand or something, I mean it isn't, but just say it is because, right, well, if it was one hundred and one: wouldn't work. Ninety-nine: wouldn't work. Has to be exactly one hundred.

Fraction more or less? Wouldn't happen.

Okay. Fluke.

But it's not just gravity. Electro-magnetism,

speed of light, rate of expansion of the universe, all of these

exactly right.

For the universe to exist like this…

Exactly.

And it's all just a bit too jammy, it's just too fucking, not to be, you know, not to be

and this is scientists saying this, not just me.

So.

Science just ignores it.

Bit irritating

but let's get on with things.

Beat.

Then comes the cosmological constant.

Basically it's a thing to do with dark matter, okay, it's something to do with Einstein coz he said well, with all this gravity and whatever what's holding the universe the way it is and they didn't really know, so he ignored it and years later it's dark matter or whatever, I don't know but the thing is

this

value

for the cosmological constant is

one in

a trillion trillion trillion, trillion trillion trillion, trillion trillion trillion

I mean it's literally like that, I'm not sure if I've got them all, but it's literally that many trillions and you have to go

oh, come on

that's no accident, that's not just luck.

You know.

So it points to

design

which means and no I'm not talking about a white beard or Allah or Buddha or you know, all of a sudden the Bible's right, but you know, I mean maybe the universe itself, I don't know and that's the thing, no-one knows but you can't just ignore it and the

scientists

well, they don't really

they're not so fond of that idea, so

and this is on the programme, this is the scientists' alternative which is

that there are an infinite number of universes

gazillions and gazillions and gazillions of universes

where every possibility is played out.

Pause.

That's it.

That is the best they could come up with.

And I just thought

Oh, really.

I mean for fuck's sake

just grow up

I mean Jesus fucking Christ, you know, just what is wrong with purpose, what's wrong with, you know, fucking belonging or

or

or just, you know, having an idea that there is something, that there is a point and that maybe it's about more than just I have this pot of stuff here and that's got more in it than your pot of stuff over there, but I'm just talking about, maybe, I dunno, choosing a world that is more than numbers and quantities and saving and choosing a world that is flesh and bone and

love or,

more than just

isn't it more than just

money, mathematics, numbers, values, I don't know

Isn't it?

Don't you think it is?

Isn't money dead? Or something?

Isn't it?

When you look around?

Don't we know that in our heart of heart of hearts?

And that we're looking for more, individually and as a, and all this, all these troubles are just symptoms of that search?

Pause.

He's asked me to marry him.

Beat.

I said yes.

We were in bed and I was playing with his mole, he has this mole on his forearm and I said you should get this checked out and he laughs and he says that's what his ex was always saying to him and I say she was right because it's dangerous and he said thinking of being with me long term then and I said, and I'm talking to his mole as I'm speaking and suddenly I'm telling him that while being with him

I have

discovered

that language is completely useless and that we only bother with it because

we haven't got telepathy

and there is no language

that can express

– this stuff is just pouring out of me –

that can express how I feel about him which is why I have to fuck him because it's the closest

I can get

to

telling him how I feel about him.

And I look up.

And he's crying.

And he's not that sort of man that cries.

And he tells me that I'd better marry him then.

And I say yes and

I

Know, he feels, the same

I know.

So maybe this is why. Why I'm, you know, why I believe there is something more.

Because I have evidence of it.

I live in it.

Beat.

Not saying I don't want things though.

She laughs.

I do. I do want things. I want things for us. I've begun to look at my life and say, well, it has been a little bit

scruffy

and now I don't want that. I want it to be a bit neater, I want it to be a bit like it's supposed to be, I want it to be a bit like

She laughs.

a bit like it is on the telly.

She laughs.

I know, I know. What a cunt.

Beat.

Right now

maybe right now I'm feeling that there has to be

something